FLASHBACKS

THE FLASHBACKS SERIES IS SPONSORED BY THE

EUROPEAN ETHNOLOGICAL RESEARCH CENTRE

CELTIC & SCOTTISH STUDIES

UNIVERSITY OF EDINBURGH

27–29 GEORGE STREET

EDINBURGH EH8 9LD

FLASHBACKS

OTHER TITLES IN THE SERIES:

The Making of *Am Fasgadh*
An Account of the Origins of the Highland Folk Museum by its Founder
Isabel Frances Grant MBE, LLD

From Kelso to Kalamazoo
The Life and Times of George Taylor 1803–1891
Edited by Margaret Jeary and Mark A. Mulhern

Showfolk
An Oral History of a Fairground Dynasty
Frank Bruce

Scotland's Land Girls
Breeches, Bombers and Backaches
Edited by Elaine M. Edwards

Galoshins Remembered
'*A penny was a lot in these days*'
Edited by Emily Lyle

FLASHBACKS

An Orkney Boyhood

Written by
Duncan Cameron Mackenzie

Edited by
Caroline Milligan and Mark A. Mulhern

in association with
THE EUROPEAN ETHNOLOGICAL RESEARCH CENTRE
AND NMS ENTERPRISES LIMITED – PUBLISHING
NATIONAL MUSEUMS SCOTLAND

GENERAL EDITOR
Alexander Fenton

Published in Great Britain in 2011 by
NMS Enterprises Limited – Publishing
NMS Enterprises Limited
National Museums Scotland
Chambers Street, Edinburgh EH1 1JF

Text © Duncan Cameron Mackenzie/
European Ethnological Research
Centre 2011

Images: all photographs
© as credited 2011

ISBN 978-1-905267-54-5

The right of Duncan Cameron
Mackenzie to be identified as the
author of this book has been asserted
by him in accordance with the Copyright, Designs and Patents Act 1988.

**British Library Cataloguing in
Publication Data**
A catalogue record of this book
is available from the British Library.

Cover design by Mark Blackadder.
Cover photograph:
    Duncan Mackenzie and friends
    at play, Scapa Flow.
    (*Source:* Duncan Mackenzie)
Internal text design by NMS
    Enterprises Limited – Publishing.
Printed and bound in Great Britain
    by Bell & Bain Limited, Glasgow.

For a full listing of related titles and
the work of the EERC, please visit:

www.nms.ac.uk/books [and]
**www.celtscot.ed.ac.uk/
    EERC_home.htl**

CONTENTS

Acknowledgements 6

List of Illustrations 7

Map of Orkney 8

Foreword by Mark A. Mulhern 9

Preface by Duncan Cameron Mackenzie 11

AN ORKNEY BOYHOOD 13

Epilogue 110

Glossary 112

ACKNOWLEDGEMENTS

ALTHOUGH a record of my own experiences this account would never have been written without the inspiration, encouragement and assistance of my family, friends and associates. Of all who were involved, the most influential and noteworthy are the following:

Vi Smith – long-term partner and friend, whom I live with in Capetown. Vi has been supportive, patient and understanding in editing and typing the final draft, guided by my notes and memories.

Nancy Spiers – Vi's mother living in Glasgow. On hearing that my own uncle had written his boyhood story of growing up, Nancy endeavoured to get me a copy of his book and presented it to me, suggesting that I follow on with my own story in a similar manner.

Fiona – my sister in Orkney. Fiona supplied me with family photos and information and kept me in touch with Orkney in general.

My brothers – Ian, Gavin and Colin – and their families, for all their advice, information and photos of events to keep my account in perspective.

Duncan Cameron Mackenzie
CAPE TOWN, SOUTH AFRICA
JANUARY 2011

LIST OF ILLUSTRATIONS

1. Burray as viewed from the top of Big Brae. The Big Brae runs down to a T-junction. The Lye Well, Eel Burn and peat area is in the low area before the houses on the right.
2. Duncan (middle) with brothers Gavin (left) and Ian (right), 1950.
3. Duncan (middle) with brothers Gavin (left) and Ian (right), 1952.
4. Duncan (right) and brother Gavin (left) on the roof of the house at Burray.
5. Duncan (front) and friends paddling in the sea at Scapa Flow, Burray with Barrier No. 4 in the background.
6. Drawing of the raft constructed and used by Duncan and friends.
7. Drawing of a 'Neepie Lantern' by Duncan Mackenzie.
8. Duncan (front row, fourth from left) with school classmates, 1954.
9. Duncan (back row, right) with school classmates, 1956.
10. Old Burray School, Duncan's first school.
11. Doull's grocery van at Burray scrap-yard.
12. Left to right – Gavin, Ian and Duncan Mackenzie, 1956.
13. Duncan (second from left) with brothers Colin, Ian and Gavin, with their cousin Nancy (left) and Vera McDonald (right).
14. 'Gowan Braes', Duncan's granny's house. Left to right – Norman and Tommy (Duncan's uncles), and Duncan's mother, a neighbour and Granny.
15. Duncan's granny, aged approximately 70 years.
16. The Lye Burn ditch from where Duncan's family used to cut peats. The peat-digging area is fenced on each side by barbed wire.
17. Burray village from the top of School Brae looking towards South Ronaldsay.
18. Burray looking towards South Ronaldsay at Barrier No. 4.
19. People fishing on Warebanks Barrier No. 3.
20. Duncan with crane engineering colleagues, South Africa, c.1992.
21. Duncan (back row, sixth from left) at work-place event, 1994.

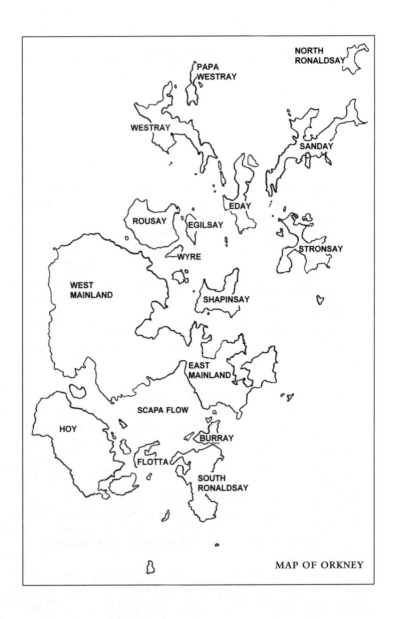

NORTH
RONALDSAY

PAPA
WESTRAY

WESTRAY

SANDAY

EDAY

ROUSAY

EGILSAY

WYRE

STRONSAY

WEST
MAINLAND

SHAPINSAY

EAST
MAINLAND

SCAPA FLOW

HOY

BURRAY

FLOTTA

SOUTH
RONALDSAY

MAP OF ORKNEY

FOREWORD

THE 'Flashbacks' series presents, in printed form, the words of individuals concerning aspects of their lives in Scotland. The content is variously composed of interview transcriptions, memoir or autobiography. The aim of the series is to gather in and re-transmit to a wider audience, fragments of the lived life.

Individually and collectively, the volumes of the 'Flashbacks' give an account of 'what a life was' in different places. These volumes do this by giving an insight into the ways in which individuals lived their lives and how they felt about those lives. By allowing people to give their own account, in their own words, the reader gains an insight to different lives in different parts of Scotland.

This particular volume gives the recollections of a lad growing up in Orkney in the 1950s. With humour and candour Duncan relates the events and habits of his childhood self which will chime with many. The fun and constraints of childhood and family life are opened up for us by an honest narrator. In the process we learn about Duncan himself and about life on Orkney in the 1950s. Whether it be scavenging the scuttled ships at Scapa Flow or fishing off the Churchill barriers, we learn of aspects of life that were, and continue to be, particular to the place. In what follows, the memories of childhood are acute and vivid, showing that the newness of experience is formative of self and place in powerful ways.

The essence of the 'Flashbacks' series is the everyday life of as broad a sample of people as possible. Everyday life is often held to be that which is lived in between interesting events, with those events constituting our stories or our histories. However, it is in the everyday that we meet most people; that we prepare and eat meals; that we raise our children and that we engage in work and other activities. In short, it is in the everyday that we live most of our lives. The accounts given in this volume add to the Flashbacks project which will continue with further volumes by different people – perhaps even you.

Mark A. Mulhern
EUROPEAN ETHNOLOGICAL RESEARCH CENTRE
EDINBURGH 2011

PREFACE

WHAT follows is my perception and experiences of life between the ages of four to fourteen. Now at the enlightened age of sixty-two, I feel detached, just enough, to reflect on where I was and what I did in my youth.

Having played, worked and learned a lot with my own son David growing up (born 8 November 1980), I got a second chance to understand and hopefully improve what I could.

Duncan Cameron Mackenzie
JANUARY 2011

THE WEDDING OF DUNCAN CHARLES MACKENZIE
AND HELEN AGNES BRUCE, 16 MAY 1945 –
DUNCAN MACKENZIE'S FATHER AND MOTHER.

AN ORKNEY BOYHOOD

WHEN I was four years old, I lived with my father, mother, two big brothers – Ian who was eight and Gavin six – on the island of Burray. I would later have a younger brother and sister, making me the middle one of five children. And although I was the middle one, it was me who was named Duncan after Dad.

I started school at four in the month of July, a few months before my fifth birthday on 17 October. There must have been a population explosion that year in Orkney, because my infant class started off with six boys and three girls. Considering the total population of the Orkney Islands was roughly 19,000, this huge influx was very unusual, although I was unaware of it at the time.

Our house was on the main road, which was within easy access to everything. Although it was not possible to travel far within the road system of Orkney, everything seemed very distant to me. This main tarmac road ran from one side of the island of Burray to the other, although definitely not in a straight line. From our house, 'Fernleigh', however, there was a flat road to the school about a hundred yards away on the crossroads. The road from the school down to the village was known as the School Brae.

This village, Wasten or 'west end', had a pier which seemed to me at that time to be as big as a harbour. In from the pier was a huge double-storey warehouse used for various sorts of storage, and part of it had been used for drying or kippering fish, or both. This building was just known as the 'big store'. There were three houses on this point, between the big store and the beach on the left side of the pier as you faced the sea.

The occupant of one of these houses was Annie 'of the point' Wylie who was old – well, over fifty. She would often walk down to the pier with her fishing rod and mackerel bait, cast a line over the end of the pier, catch one or two big cod or sea trout, then pack up and go back home – all in half an hour. My brothers and I, on the other hand, had been fishing there for hours, catching nothing bigger than four-inch sillocks. We would sometimes talk to Annie, emphasising that in the general scheme of things this didn't seem right or fair. If we put on a really good performance and appeared really disappointed or envious, she took pity on us and gave over some of her mackerel bait, sometimes even a whole fish. Although the mackerel bait was better than the cockles or limpets we used, we still never caught any of the really big fish. And to make matters worse, Sandy Wylie the shopowner– another 'fogey' over fifty – who also came down to the slipway at low-tide, often proceeded to spear about a dozen flounders where we were fishing; though we had caught one or two with our fishing lines, the rest just sat there waiting to get speared.

There was no way we were going to accept that the fogeys were better at catching fish than us, so something must have been wrong in our universe when all this was happening.

Another inhabitant of the three houses was young Sandy (Alexander) Wylie, who was probably related to Annie. (Orkney was either limited in people's names or they liked their names so much that every generation got the same name.) Anyway, this Sandy Wylie was only in his mid-twenties and a sort of student teacher, and he became our Sunday School teacher for a while.

The third house was where Marshall and Marcus Kidd lived with their mother. The brothers went to school with us. We never saw their father. I never knew what happened, but in Orkney in these situations it was just assumed that they didn't have a father, which on reflection now is all a bit strange.

Next to the big store was a fenced-in coal-yard. Although it had a gate secured with chain and padlock, it wasn't particularly thief-proof. But no one seemed to steal any coal – well, not openly anyway.

The coal always arrived by ship at the pier. When it docked, we would rush down to the pier to watch all the unloading and trucking going on. Then, once the coal was loaded up and transported to the coal-yard, we would search through the coal mountains to collect the highly prized yellow insulated copper blasting wire. It was always there, if you knew where to look.

After losing its cargo of coal, the ship was usually re-loaded with a cargo of sand for its return journey. This sand was excavated from our special quarry, about a third of a mile from the pier. The sand was pure white and very clean, and in great demand for building and construction work.

In the village there was a Presbyterian Kirk and manse, three shops, a post office, bakery, boat-building yard and a village hall – more than enough to keep everyone busy.

From the age of four onwards, I spent much of my time walking to the shops, armed with a shopping bag, a list and a ration book. Because World War II had seriously depleted supplies and resources – including food – we were limited as to what we could buy and ration books were issued. The ration system was based solely on foodstuff, irrespective of price and how much money you had. Meat and sugar were two of the items that I particularly recall, but I think it affected everything to varying degrees. This rationing seemed to continue until I was about eight.

Although from home to the village was about two-thirds of a mile, it never appeared very far or too difficult, even loaded down with a big bag of groceries.

I always went to the shop every Thursday for *The Orcadian*, the weekly newspaper. My father and mother would read the local news, often having great discussions about it. As children we were never particularly interested. Every weekend, *The Orcadian* was ceremoniously wrapped up and marked 'newspaper only' and duly posted off to my mother's sister Molly in

London – presumably to keep her and her family up-to-date with all the interesting and exciting activities she was missing by being stuck out of the way in the big city.

Molly Bruce married and became Mrs French. She had two kids – Marion, who was about Ian's age, and Alex whose age was somewhere between Gavin and myself. They came to visit us once in Burray when I was about five or six. Although my mother always kept in touch with her sister, we children, despite being first cousins, never did.

On Saturdays, Ian, Gavin or myself would go to the shop. Sometimes, two of us would go together. Saturday shopping was the highlight of the week, when we got *The Beano*, *Dandy*, *Topper* and *Beezer* comics. My mother's favourite was *The People's Friend*, along with *The Mirror* or *Daily Record* for national news.

Even with all our village shops, we still had back-up by way of vans and mobile shops. These included Wylie's shop van, which you entered at the front side door and up two steps. Some of the other vans you went in at the back door, while the driver/shopkeeper got out of the driver's seat and put down a hinged counter-top. As far as we were concerned, you could buy just about anything from the van that you could from the shop, but we only had Wylie's van once a week. Somehow the vans must have co-ordinated their days, because we always had Guthrie the butcher on Saturday (from St Margaret's Hope in the South Ronaldsay island); our own Wylie's Burray shop van came on Tuesday; Robertson's from St Margaret's Hope on Wednesday; and the Co-operative, also from the Hope, came on Thursday. A Co-operative fish van from Kirkwall, our capital on the main island, came on Friday. Ironically we were always buying fish from this van, even though we were out trying to catch fish ourselves all the time. Maybe the fish from the Co-op was better – they were at least a more dependable supply.

We also had a mobile library van on Monday, with its amazing collection of books and gramophone records. This library van also came over from Kirkwall, from the main library there. The post office van seemed to go around every day except Sundays which, although it was the official Royal Mail, was run locally by a family of father, mother, son and daughter. The mother seemed to run the actual post office, assisted by her daughter on rare occasions. The father drove the red Royal Mail van and the son went around on the Royal Mail bicycle with his leather mail bag, delivering letters and small parcels. Both the father and son wore their official dark blue Royal Mail uniforms and peaked caps with great pride and a sense of importance, and they were never belittled or trifled with.

Even the big parcels were hand-delivered to the door and had to be signed for. Some were the dreaded C.O.D. (cash on delivery). My father told me the ones you didn't have to pay for were C.I.A. (cash in advance) – presumably paid for by the person who sent them.

Although the road down to the village and past the school was known as the School Brae, that was the direction when we ventured out and turned left into the road. When we turned right into the road, then we went in the direction of the Big Brae. This road to the Big Brae was past the peat bog and river. The river was actually a burn about two foot wide, which ran in a direct straight line north to south. The burn had its source in Etna Loch, very close to the north shore of Burray, and flowed from the loch at the north shore under the road into the sea, thereby travelling in a northerly direction. It also ran in a southerly direction out of the other side of the loch all the way across the island and into the sea on the south shore. Approximately half-way from the loch to the south shore was a natural bubbling spring known as the Lye Well. This spring always produced clear, pure, running water and was safe to drink all year round. It also fed into the burn running towards the south shore, on our side of the island. If at any time the drinking water was unavailable from any other wells, the Lye could always be depended on and never ran dry. (Bottled drinking water hadn't been invented yet.)

At the south shore end of the burn, closest to where we lived,

Ian, Gavin and me – and sometimes Ruthie – would set out on our adventures. Ruthie – Ruth Douglas – lived two houses away at the Douglas Esso garage, and was about the same age as Ian. Ruthie seemed to join in a lot of our activities about this time, and for three to four years thereafter until she went to the High School.

One of our main activities was spending time at the Eel Burn. We used to dam up the burn and use it as a pond to keep fish, eels and crabs, sea urchins, starfish, sand shrimps and hermit crabs, which we caught with nets and fishing rods. The dam was built only of stones and sea-sand; and even with all our ingenious system of overflow, it usually only lasted about a day before the tide came in and flattened it, probably to the great relief of the fish and other sea-creatures we were holding prisoner. We always referred to this burn as Eel Burn because we caught small conger eels there, ranging from two inches to a foot in length. Some of those eels grew up to three foot long and we would watch them when they came out of the loch, wriggling across the road towards the sea at the north shore. We never risked catching these larger eels though.

The road over this burn, on the south shore (our side), past the peat bog, was called the Big Brae. Although the island wasn't excessively hilly, this brae was definitely too long and steep for anyone to cycle up. However, because we had the two braes we could get involved in other activities, such as trolley-racing in the good weather and sledging during the winter snow and ice. The sledging was definitely slower and a bit safer.

The trolley-racing was quite simple – four wheels, ingenious steering-bar, no brakes and maximum speed to the bottom of the hill, unless some mishap intervened. If you survived the race and were still capable of the long haul back, then you went to the top to try again. All this rough road stuff was carried out at speed on a very good tarmac road, often at night with no vehicle or streetlights, and usually in the middle of the local traffic – well, about six to eight vehicles an hour. Nonetheless, we managed to survive without any major disasters.

The weather is never very good on Orkney, although the four seasons seemed to be well defined. Summer – June, July and August, 20–22°C – was a great time of the year, with six weeks of school holidays, and quite warm and sunny some days. Daylight lasted from about four in the morning to after midnight, sometimes beginning as early as two. Autumn – that is, September, October and November – was cold, wet and windy, with rough seas. Winter – December, January and February – brought rain, wind, hail, snow and ice, often mixed with thunder and lightning. Then in spring – March, April and May – all the snow melts and the flowers break through. Orkney, however, is constantly windy – with only the speed and intensity varying.

Sundays were completely different to the rest of the week, with well-defined rules. Get up in the morning, get dressed, and head out to church. Clothing was similar to school uniform – the boys wore short trousers, while older boys and adults wore longs. All three of us – Ian, Gavin and myself – would walk past the school and down the School Brae to Sunday School at the Kirk. Being good Presbyterians our attendance was taken for granted, every Sunday without fail from ten to eleven o'clock. The big Kirk service was from half eleven until one, which we sometimes had to attend if there was some special service on, for example at Christmas, Easter and Harvest-time Thanksgiving. Then it was back up the School Brae and home.

Dinner on Sunday was at half past one; if we had dinner in the evening on any other day, it was still called dinner. This was the main meal, irrespective of the time of day. The three of us and my mother and father sat around the table. Sunday dinner was always a roast – with no exception – usually pot roast beef; although we always kept our own hens, roast chicken was only eaten on occasion. Everything was dished up from the table – mashed potatoes, roast potatoes, mashed turnip, peas or cabbage, and gravy. The dessert was sponge pudding and custard, or fruit and jelly, or rice pudding (rice was always dessert for us, never savoury).

During this dinner the only drink allowed was water, and

after dinner only tea, never coffee. Tea was always of the tea-leaf type – either Brooke Bond, Lipton's or Typhoo – in a teapot. I didn't even know that tea-bags existed. Coffee was only for eleven o'clock on Saturday. Maybe other days as well, but we were at school so I don't know. But for whoever happened to be at home at exactly eleven on Saturday morning, the ritual was always the same – kettle of boiling water on the table, tin of Nescafé coffee, tin of Carnation evaporated milk, bowl of sugar, cups and saucers (never mugs), teaspoons, and a packet of Crawford's custard creams or McVitie's chocolate digestives. Those of us who were there at the time, and our parents, sometimes just our mother, sat around the table with the coffee and biscuits, then my mother and father would smoke – just as a matter of course, as most people smoked in those days.

On Sunday afternoons by about half two, all this eating and talking was finished up and the three of us brothers then went for our long walk around the square. This was compulsory. The walk was in fact a major trek and we only did it in good weather, which meant anything other than snow or rain.

Since we lived in the middle of one side of the square, we could either walk towards the school or the other way over the Eel Burn and up the Big Brae. The long walk never seemed to need much discussion and the general consensus was always up the Big Brae. A split decision of two going in one direction and one going in the other was never even considered. So off we'd go, over the Eel Burn bridge and up the Big Brae, passing the open ditches on both sides of the road designed to collect rainwater run-off from the road. They usually had some water running in them, ending up in the burn on the way to the sea.

We only passed one house at the bottom of the Brae, and this house, with its perfect garden and everything else always well-kept, belonged to a really elderly couple. Now, to us anyone over forty appeared old, but I'm sure this couple must have been over sixty. The woman was always known just as Betsie, and she had completely white hair. Every day, except Sunday, she would walk to the shop – in all weather – with her shopping basket. To us,

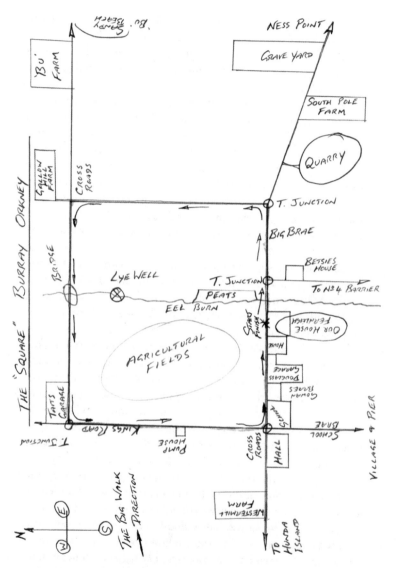

SKETCH OF THE 'LONG WALK AROUND THE SQUARE' ON BURRAY,
BY DUNCAN MACKENZIE

there was no real need to walk to the shop every day, a round trip that was quite a fair distance, so this must have been a way of getting exercise or meeting people, or whatever. And she always walked alone, never with her husband. Even the young people used to remark on how fit she was.

Along the rest of the road was open fields with barbed-wire fences. The fields had mainly cattle, sheep, or occasionally a horse or two in them. Depending on the time of the year, they might have a crop of oats or barley or root crops of tatties or neeps, and sometimes haystacks. The sheep would lean or rub themselves against the barbed wire and wool would come off and get caught on the fence. We would gather this wool fleece for no good reason other than there was a nice feel to it, and as we continued along the road we would let the wool blow away through our fingers.

The four sides of the square combined meant that the total trek was somewhere around two and a half miles of good tarmac roads. At the top of the Brae we turned left, which meant going north, although we never particularly thought of it from a geographical point of view.

Along the sides of the road and along the open ditches there were the usual types of wildflowers – or weeds, as we usually regarded them. There were the very bright, yellow dandelions. When you picked the flower, the stem was hollow like a straw, with white milk sap which you could dab onto your skin – or preferably someone else's skin. The sap would instantly turn black. There was also the three-leafed clover. I don't think we ever found ones with four leaves, although there was always plenty of talk about this mystical and elusive plant. Anyway, the clover that we found grew in abundance, and although the leaves looked the same the flowers were either a definite red or white – these flowers we called 'curly doddies'. Then there were the nice, white daisies with the bright yellow centres. When we were four or five, we made these into daisy chains after being taught by our mother – we were quite expert at this. There was also the bright yellow buttercup flowers which you could pick and hold under each other's chins. If you got a reflection from that person's chin, it meant they were good and didn't tell lies. If you didn't get a reflection, they were definitely bad and not to be trusted. So we had our own organically indigenous lie detectors long before they were invented by the boffins, presumably at great expense. The older folk would tell us that the bulb roots of buttercups were good to eat, so of course I had to try this. I dug up a buttercup root, which looked like a small onion about the size of a marble, and although I don't really like onions, this tasted much worse – and very bitter. So my buttercup-tasting days came to an abrupt end.

There were also cocks-and-hens, low lawn flowers, a mixture of red and yellow. And our favourites – dandelions – which you could pick and blow the little parachute seeds all over the place, and even onto each other. We no doubt managed to spread the dandelion population far and wide by our antics. Although most people regarded dandelions, daisies and curly doddies as weeds, most of them had a very nice smell that was as good as any scent or perfume that my mother used to keep in her bottles.

I also remember white marsh-lilies, like Arum or St Joseph lilies I suppose, but they were not very plentiful. As we got stuck in the swamp mud trying to get to them, they were usually left undisturbed.

We also had our fair share of nettles, thistles and some sort of prickly gorse bush. The nettles were fine with small violet flowers, and if left alone were no problem. However, we couldn't leave well alone and would invariably get stung by having nettle fights, although we did have our own antidote to nettle stings – the juice of the local dock leaf which worked even better than calamine lotion. The thistles, often with a beautiful display of purple flowers, were also better left alone for the same reason as nettles. The gorse bushes too, with their tiny orange berries and thousands of spikes and thorns were just too difficult to get through, so nothing ever happened to them.

The other favourite was the 'sticky wullie' plant, which was great fun. We would collect as many sticky wullies as possible and throw them at each other. The more you could stick on your opponent, the better.

Occasionally we would encounter several areas with the blue, white and pink bells of hyacinths, daffodils, crocuses, snow-drops, pansies and violets. These usually grew after being discarded or dumped out of someone's garden. Or perhaps they were strategically planted by some caring person with an environmental vision well ahead of their time.

It was possible to go straight on at the three-way junction at the top of the Brae. If you did so, you got to the old, now dis-used, stone quarry on the right, which was full of water like a small loch. Past this quarry on the right was the farm called South Pole where John Laird, also in my class, lived. There was also a North Pole Farm. On past South Pole, almost as far as the Ness Point, was the cemetery. Although this was a very old graveyard with the ancient broken-down stone ruins of a build-ing, there had been burials in Burray at the kirkyard itself even before this cemetery had been established. I would sometimes go to this graveyard with my granny, mother and brothers, and put flowers in the pots and vases of some of our deceased relatives. We would then go around looking at the old grave-stones and statues, checking on names and dates. It was all quite interesting – we never really thought of the residents as dead people.

Our long square walk continued north with a slight downhill slope, again one or two houses, with many open fields, and on the next corner was actually a crossroads. Our route, however, involved a left turn going downhill, heading west to the bridge over the burn, with its stone dykes (walls) on either side.

Straight across was up to Gallow Hill Farm, where Anne, James and Maureen Laird lived with their father and mother. James was in the same class as me at school (although he was apparently not related to John Laird). To the right was Bu Farm where Billy Das lived, and if you continued on you came to the nice sandy Bu Beach. Billy Das seems to have been famous, at least by Orkney standards, for three things. One, he was bald at thirty; two, he had the first television set in Burray, perhaps even first in Orkney; and three, he had a speed boat and travelled around the various waterways just speeding or water-skiing, or both.

We now walked uphill towards Tait's Garage on the corner, which was a T-junction running into King's Road. Then we took a left turn again, heading south towards the school corner, half-way along King's Road, where there was a small concrete pump house with an exhaust chimney sticking out of the roof. Often when we walked past, the diesel engine would be chugging away. This pump house was a small structure with its four sides about six and a half feet high with a flat roof and a small door. In spite of trying, I never ever got inside. We presumed it was a pump taking water from the Lye well spring up to Westermill Farm.

Tait's Garage was owned by Alfie and Johnny Tait's father and uncle. Alfie was Ian's friend and Johnny was Alfie's older brother who used to drive the articulated lorry. As kids we sometimes got in the back of the lorry and just travelled around until it came back to the garage, sometimes two or three, even as much as six, hours later.

The other thing I remember about Tait's Garage was the day I needed new brake pads for my bike. Alfie told me they supplied and could fit them. At the age of eight or nine, I thought that was a good idea and gave them my bike to fix, which I collected the next day with brand new brakes all round. This, however, cost over £2 which I didn't have, so I told my mother what had happened. She told me Alfie had conned me into the job. I should have just bought the brake parts and fixed it myself – which I have done ever since. My mother reluctantly gave me the £2 to pay Tait's Garage, and I think I had to pay back this vast sum. I'm still not sure whether she was more annoyed with me or with Alfie.

I also fixed other bits of my bike myself and this included broken drive-chains and doing repairs with my John Bull puncture repair kit. I wouldn't be caught out by Alfie Tait again.

Anyway we continued along to the school corner and turned

left again, going east now in along our own road past the school, and past the William Douglas Esso Garage where Ruthie lived. The Douglas Garage, which repaired vehicles, bikes and anything else, also supplied diesel, petrol and paraffin. It had a small, very limited shop, which, among other things, sold fags, matches and lemonade. Douglas's was also the home of the local diesel-driven electrical power station.

Once past the garage, we were the second house on the right, and finally home. All this took just over an hour.

* * *

It seemed to me as a boy that all utilities and amenities seemed to work just fine in Orkney – or at least in the small area that I knew, the island of Burray. We had good roads, hot and cold running water, electricity, coal and peat fireplaces, and a telephone. The phone was in fact a public telephone in one of the old-fashioned red G.P.O. boxes, strategically positioned outside the post office in the village. A few people had private or party-line telephones, but not many, and it didn't seem much of a priority. Communication seemed to work perfectly well without them.

The electricity, however, was a completely different story. Up until I was four or five, our power station was the Douglas Garage where Mr Douglas had a diesel engine generator unit which he ran from eight to twelve hours a day. This appeared to supply the school, and a lot of houses and shops in and around the village, and it was used mainly for lights. Most cooking and heating was by coal, wood or peat, on fireplaces and stoves which people kept burning from six o'clock in the morning until twelve midnight.

When the power station was off, we used oil lamps – either a glass or metal lamp – with an adjustable wick filled with paraffin. The lit wick was shielded by another, removable, glass cylinder. This lamp gave off a light equivalent to about four to six candles. Our other form of lighting was the Tilley lamp, also fuelled with paraffin. Gas never seemed to be an option, although the Tilley worked exactly like a gas lamp. When it was pumped up to the correct pressure, a valve was slowly released and a burner soaked in methylated spirit was lit and clipped on under the mantle. As the mantle fired up, it created a terrific dazzling white glow at least as good as a hundred-watt electric light bulb.

Now, for cooking emergencies, when the peat stove wasn't lit or not up to temperature and the power station was off, we had Primus stoves. The Primus stove was similar to the Tilly lamp, except it had a permanent circular dish for the methylated spirit which was lit to heat the burner head before releasing the pressurised paraffin. Then, *presto*, you got a hot, roaring burner, very similar to a modern gas stove. This could boil a kettle of water in less than ten minutes. I don't think electric kettles had been invented yet, but even if they had been we had nothing to plug it into anyway.

Whether electric irons had been invented or not was also irrelevant, for precisely the same reason. There were two types of irons. One was a totally solid metal unit which looked like a modern iron, but was heated up by sitting on top of the stove. The other type was similar in looks, but hollow inside. It had a sliding access hatch which was opened, and a red-hot triangular, solid metal block was loaded into the hatch giving an instant iron which stayed hot for a long time.

When I was about six years of age we experienced an electrical revolution. There was a great flurry of activity all over the island, as huge wooden poles were erected along the road and across the links. We even got one just outside our back door. Suddenly there were copper cables strung out across the tops of the poles, and feeders going into all the houses – even cables laid under the sea from island to island. Now we had real electricity twenty-four hours a day, seven days a week, for lights and plugs. We got a four-plate electric cooker with an eye-level grill and oven, and an electric kettle and electric iron. All the things we didn't know we needed, we suddenly had.

This electrical revolution changed everything, presumably for the better, except for one thing. I now had to spend days up in the loft space pulling wires and cables around, and feeding them through holes in the ceiling and down walls, while my father connected up all sorts of new lights, switches and plugs. After a month or so of all this electrical work and fitting brackets and clips for the cables in the loft, things eased off a bit and got more or less back to normal. The plus side was I could wait and get up fifteen minutes before school and still make a cup of tea without being late. We now had lights that worked, at any time of the day or night.

As far as the water system was concerned, we had two main supplies. The soft water supply came from the rainwater collected from the roof by spoots and guided down pipes into tanks (no roof water ever reached the ground). This soft water was used for personal washing, clothes and dishwashing only. The other, hard water, came out of the ground: this was for drinking and cooking, for the hens' feed and for other livestock. Like the soft water, the hard water was private and individual to each household.

Our own hard water came from a well of about twenty-six feet deep. Now as fate would have it, one very dry summer this well dried up; or what really happened was that the water at the bottom of the well was too low – or the suction pipe was too short. Being the smallest and readily available at the time – lucky me – I became an instant aqua-expert and plumber. A rope was tied around my middle and I was lowered into the bowels of the well to investigate and fix the problem. This seemed to be regarded as run-of-the-mill procedure, so I thought in an effort not to disappoint anyone, now that I was the newly appointed aqua-expert, I had better get this situation under control. On reaching the bottom I discovered it was mainly soft, soggy sand and not much water. I loosened off the pipe, which wasn't really fixed to much, and guided it from the well while it was pulled out (by my father and brothers) for inspection, cleaning and maintenance.

My main job now, with a bucket and trowel which had been lowered down on the pipe rope, was to dig the sand out of the bottom of the well and fill the bucket, which was then pulled up and emptied. Although this wasn't particularly hard work, it was a bit cramped and dark, and not the ideal location to be in. Several buckets of soggy sand later, I declared the well completely clear of all loose sand, and demanded out.

Although the excavations were officially over, I now had pipe-positioning work to see to. The refurbished and all-clean galvanised steel pipe, which I think had been extended by adding an extra bit on the end, was now lowered back down the well. This pipe had a filter-sieve thing fitted at the bottom end, but I still had to settle this on top of a concrete block in the water at the bottom of the well. The water was now almost knee-deep. I suppose to anyone else, a six-year-old's knee-deep is not a lot of water, but when you are the six-year-old who is cramped and at the bottom of a dark well, and in rising water up to your knees, it appears dangerously deep. When I completed the mission, I requested an immediate escape. With much screaming and shouting, and after some sort of committee meeting up at the earth level, and with me having to confirm all was proper and correct in the bowels of the planet, I was hoisted up and set free.

All the pipes and pumps and things were then connected up by my father and brothers and I was instantly demoted from aqua-expert to general 'gofer'. Eventually, with one hand-pump outside at the top of the well and another fitted onto the end of the kitchen sink, everything was ready. The pumps were primed with a bucket of water and after much vigorous pumping, they both worked.

At first the water was a bit muddy, but by the next day it was pure clear spring water and it remained like that – so I never had to go back into the bowels of the earth again.

Although Burray is a small island, about two miles by three miles, surrounded by sea, and having a loch and a quarry full of water which rarely if ever runs dry, fresh water was never a plentiful commodity to be taken for granted. However, when I was about ten, we had a water revolution. This consisted of having new mainline pipes laid in trenches along the roads throughout Burray and, I think, South Ronaldsay as well – by the Orkney County Council. Once the mainline pipes were in and the trenches covered up and all back to normal, then each individual house was connected. Once connected, the water pressure was amazing when compared to our soft-water gravity feed from the roof tanks. This new Council water had ten times the pressure and made all our roof tanks obsolete. Although I think you could drink this new water, and use it for cooking, we never did – and we kept our hard-water well and pump.

But, like the electrical revolution, the water revolution also caused upheaval. Whereas all electrics were done within the roof-space, all water works had to be arranged under the floor. The way to get under the floor was to remove the solid concrete block manhole cover situated in the concrete slab outside the coal cellar, then to go down into the dungeon armed with a torch, Stillson spanners, monkey wrenches, and special string and paste for pipe joints. After crawling around under the floor for a few weeks, and periodically having to go back down to carry out some minor adjustments, the new water system was declared a vast improvement on the rainwater and gravity feed system. These were now obsolete and the old system was dismantled and broken down over time, although Mum remained adamant that this new water was nowhere near as good as rainwater for washing her hair.

At the other end of the water supply, so to speak, was the drains and sewerage system. The drains from the kitchen sink and bathroom were quite straightforward, and the sink, basin and bath water ran out through the usual u-bends and traps and out into the ground via a soak-away area. This seemed to add all sorts of nutrients, and the grass really was greener in this area. The septic tank and sewerage system was completely different, however. This was a major concrete construction in an underground pit with all sorts of in-flow and out-flow levels and traps, with a three-foot square concrete slab cover. This was situated half-way between the house and the shed. There was a major drainpipe system on the out-flow side, with ten-inch diameter pipes that ran underground – the full length of the property – towards the links and the sea. Through evaporation or leakage, only a trickle of almost pure, clear water ever reached the end of the drainpipe at the links end – in the wild grass, nettles and gorse bushes. This was at a time when it was quite acceptable to have sewerage drains running directly into the sea.

The material that always seemed to be in use was cement in its various forms. There were mixtures of cement and sand for block-building and plastering; we also had cement, sand and stones, or stone chips, for making concrete blocks and other structural stuff. All this meant a great deal of mixing, which was usually done on a concrete slab with hundredweight bags of dry-powder cement, sand, water, and with or without stones – all in varying amounts depending on what it was for and how strong it had to be. This sometimes involved ingenious reinforcing with the likes of wire mesh or steel bars, again depending on size and shape.

The mixing process would be started off by combining the correct quantities of dry powder cement with dry sand. Even the type of sand varied according to its designed purpose. It could be dug out of the sand quarry for building or plaster work, or we could use rougher stuff from the beach for concrete. With the cement and sand mixed on the slab, using a spade to drag it into a small hill, a hole was made in the centre, like a small volcano. Then water was added and mixed through, during which the water had to be blocked from running all over the place. Once the exact consistency was achieved, as calculated and advised by the experts and supervisors (of which there was never any shortage), it was time to add the stones or chips as necessary.

During all the cement-making I was involved in, which was always just cement or concrete, the word 'mortar' did not exist in my vocabulary. We always made concrete blocks using our own moulds. We later discovered that cement dye or colouring was available in various hues such as green, orange, blue and red, and – as usual – we had to give this a go. When it came to making the slab over our septic tank, we added a green dye. The slab came out greener, at least when compared to common grey cement – and it blended in with the surrounding grass.

Our house was built on half an acre of ground. The house faced the main road with a small lawn in front onto the pavement. The back door faced towards the sea. Both the front and back doors had three huge surround-type concrete steps down to what was totally flat, level ground. The doors were always painted a sort of emerald green gloss and the window frames were always white. The house was built with concrete blocks, wooden floors that you could crawl around under, and dry-wall interior partitions made of gypsum or plaster-board sheets, nailed onto wooden frames. The ceilings were constructed in a similar way.

All the interior doors were wood-panel types with mortise locks. The two outside doors were very solid and at least four inches thick with mortise and Yale locks, although the back door seemed to be permanently open, at least during daytime. The windows were wooden, and hinged on the right or left side for opening – although some were later changed to sliding horizontally, left to right. This was a good idea but, because of my father's over-the-top heavy timber construction, very difficult to operate.

Most of the roof was made from corrugated galvanised steel, painted red. There were flat concrete and tar roofs over the bathroom and front and back porch, all with skylights.

The general lay-out of the house was this. Starting at the back door and leading into the scullery, was a huge cupboard along one wall with sliding doors (much later the scullery would have a four-plate oven and grill electric cooker). Opposite this cupboard was a door to the boiler-room with three concrete steps down to the coal/wood-fired boiler for central heating (we never used peats in this boiler fire). The boiler seemed to burn and steam away permanently, although I think it must have been turned off for a few months during the summer months. The other door from this scullery led to another sort of small scullery, with a sliding door leading from there to the coal cellar which was stacked with coal from a hatch on the outside wall. The coal cellar also contained kindling wood to light the fire. However, peats were never stored in the coal cellar. This cellar had shelves, which held an old enamel teapot full of paraffin for lighting the fire, and a yellow insect spray pump which could be loaded with D.D.T. – or anything available at the time depending on the ferocity of the bugs in question. There were also various brushes, dustpans, shovels and other garden tools, as well as dusters, rags, brushes, and black and brown Kiwi shoe polish and a jar of whitening for our sand-shoes. There was also a huge cone-shaped fire extinguisher and asbestos fire blanket.

This coal cellar was also the official residence of the cats, when they were at home; it also doubled as their maternity ward. This was an arrangement that suited the cats, and humans were rarely involved in these arrangements except – unfortunately – when it came to cat population control. If the latest census figures were at a maximum of six then, unless a kitten could be given away, or it was given a special reprieve – which could only be for reasons of colouring or being extra furry, or something exceptional – then population control procedures were set in motion.

By the time I was seven or eight, I was somehow promoted to Chief Executioner, and since it was just assumed that I knew what I was doing, the only discussion that ever took place was about the deed itself.

My *modus operandi* was one of two procedures, depending on my thoughts at the time – but both involved drowning. The first involved putting the victims into a sack weighted with a big stone which I then carried all the way to the middle of the causeway barrier and threw into the sea. The sack always sank quickly and, although I was quite sad, there was little remorse to be honest. Even after I got a bike, I always walked on these missions, and always alone.

Although perhaps more obvious, my second system, either through discussion or ingenuity, I only devised much later. This involved filling a bucket with water and then taking each victim, one at a time, and holding it under water until it went lifeless. This usually involved three or four kittens each time.

I would then arrange a special funeral for the kittens, which was sometimes a mass grave or sometimes just individual graves, with small wooden crosses or gravestone monuments.

Anyway, back to the house. Moving from this small scullery and left into the main house, was what nowadays may be referred to as an open-plan living area – although it wasn't really. It was in fact a big room and the main living area for everything. There was the fireplace stove, used for all heating and cooking, and which had an easy chair placed at each side. Above the stove was a clothes pulley – two long wooden poles connected at each end with wood and three or four long ropes in between, where the washing from the outside line was hung for its final drying and airing.

On the same wall as the fireplace was a safe, which was a brick and concrete cupboard with a hinged, thick wooden door built into the outside wall – for perishables and cold food. It functioned incredibly well. This safe always had a bottle of Haig whisky in it, along with other less important stuff. When facing the fireplace, the right-hand wall had a large window, and a sideboard with all sorts of photos and candlesticks and ornaments on it. It also contained drawers with cutlery, and a cupboard door at each end housing jam, marmalade, butter, salt and pepper and sauce in the one side and all my mother's knitting and sewing stuff in the other end.

The wall opposite also had a large window and two sinks with a wringer or mangle in the middle between them, a draining-board worktop at the right-hand side, and the spring well water hand-pump at the end. Each sink also had a hot and cold water tap. The left-hand sink was only used for washing clothes, and the right-hand sink for everything else from preparing food, washing dishes, washing anything else, and often for us to wash our hands. Under the two sinks were cupboards with wooden doors where all sorts of detergents were kept – especially Tide, Lux and Fairy Liquid for clothes-cleaning and dish-washing (these were also used for our bubble-blowing games). Other soaps and shoe polish, brushes, floor polish and all sorts of household stuff were kept here too; even toilet paper, which was the hard white standard variety, and the new soft type which was always pink. The jack for removing boots was also kept here.

In the middle of the floor was a huge, wooden table, eight chairs and cushions.

All the ceilings in the house were painted either white or a very light cream. Most of the walls had wallpaper, except for those in the bathroom, kitchen and around the sinks. This wall-paper, which usually had a border along the top, was papered over periodically, for various reasons. These could be practical – because the paper was faded, badly-marked or worn here and there – or down to someone's whim for a change of scenery.

Anyway, from this main living area, a door on the back wall opposite the fireplace led to the peedie lobby (small was always referred to as 'peedie', and only Dad used the word 'wee'). Along this lobby or passage, first on the left was the lumber room which was always known as the 'glory hole'. This room had steps down to the floor and contained all sorts of books, suitcases stacked around, with coats and shopping bags hanging up. The lobby also had a row of clothes hooks along one wall with coats and jackets permanently hanging there – in no particular order. Next on the left was the bathroom, complete with a bath, wash basin and toilet, window, skylight, mirror and locking wooden door. On the right-hand side of the lobby, exactly in the middle, was the door to our room where Ian, Gavin and myself slept. This door had a pane of frosted glass at the top to give some light into the lobby. Our room had a large window, a wardrobe and cupboard, a chest of drawers and two beds, one single and one double. The sleeping arrangements were therefore one in the single and two in the double bed. Who was in the single and who was in the double varied from time to time, for no partic-ular reason.

The end of the lobby led straight into our parents' bedroom, which had two large windows, a grate, two wooden wardrobes with mirrors, a double bed, a dressing table with three hinged mirrors, and a stool. At the end of the peedie lobby, before going straight into our parents' bedroom, there was a sort of landing square open on the right side, leading into the big lobby. This big lobby was about the same length as the peedie lobby – but twice as wide. Both the big lobby and the peedie lobby had hatches in the ceiling to gain access into the loft.

At the start end of the big lobby was a huge storage cupboard for all sorts of blankets, toys and any other household equip-ment and provisions. Off to the right was the sitting room, com-plete with two windows and a grate (or fireplace), a polished rectangular expanding wooden table with six chairs, a couch/settee, two easy chairs, a dresser with a worktop and shelves, and drawers in the base unit. There was also a big cupboard built into the wall.

At the other end of the big lobby was a glass door leading to the front porch. This porch was never used for anything in particular, but it had a very big window which always seemed warm and sunny in the afternoon. It did have a table, however, with plants and flowers growing in it, and, of course, it was the way to the front door, complete with its brass letterbox. When I used to keep white mice, I had them in a cage in the front porch because it was so warm and sunny.

The house also had central heating radiators which were supplied from the boiler house – with all the pipes running under the wooden floors.

I recall, when I was nine or ten, I was given a fretwork kit for Christmas. This consisted of a green and rather odd-looking fretwork saw, a pump-action drill that looked like a screwdriver, five or six spare blades for the saw, a v-shaped chrome plate with a screw clamp and various patterns or templates, and the usual instructions. Naturally I diligently got to work, which entailed commandeering a card table, approximately two and a half feet square by the same high, which, according to the instructions, was the ideal size for my operation. The v-chrome plate was then clamped onto one side of the table and, according to the instructions, the idea was to sit at the table in front of the v, with saw in hand and a board of thin plywood – or similar – and cut shapes in the board whilst using the v as a support. So all this got set up in the big lobby, and at night – or if it was a day of rain or snow – I got into fretworking.

After using the patterns that came with the kit, I branched out and improvised my own, which included all sorts of animals like elephants, buffalo, lions and crocodiles, even dinosaurs. All my fret stuff was created with a fifth-of-an-inch-thick plywood from tea-chests which I used to beg and scrounge from the shop. If I got my timing right and they were either re-packing or throwing out, or getting in a new batch of stuff, I got lucky and got a chest.

Anyway, a fifth-of-an-inch-thick dinosaur would not stand upright for long on its feet, so I made stands for all the animals, flowers, even aircraft, cars and trains – or anything else that I could find pictures of and cut out and stick onto my plywood. Soon there were dozens of fretwork models of ingenious design all over the place.

However, what with all the cold and wet weather and long dark nights, I realised that I was neglecting my shooting practice. My first slug-gun was the o.177 calibre, and instead of using slugs or darts I decided to use lollipop sticks. These were round like a drinking straw and approximately four inches long and made of wood – perfect for what I had in mind. And so all my dinosaurs, crocodiles and elephants eventually got used for target-practice, and they got shot to pieces. This was no big deal since I just made more and varied the replacement targets to suit. But as all this target-practice took place inside the big lobby, the hit rate was getting monotonously good, so I had to vary my ammunition by cutting the lollipop sticks in half-lengths, and reduce the size of the wildlife targets. Theoretically, this should have improved my accuracy, but all that really happened was I had to pay more attention to what I was doing.

It wasn't all violence and destruction, however, because I did use my fretwork kit to make some ornamental pieces, in particular a letter- or document-holder to hang on the wall, and a jewellery box. I also stained and varnished all my works of art, some of which may be around to this day.

*   *   *

Outside the house at the back, facing the sea, we had a shed which was a twenty-foot corrugated-iron construction with four walls, a door, window, and a roof. This was the main general workshop which was always in a shambles, with nothing ever in its rightful place. Any box or drawer could contain anything – or nothing – depending on your luck or, more likely, whoever was last there. However, anything could be made or fixed in this shed, from watches to clocks, bikes to electrical gadgets, even engines.

Everything that could roost (rust) in Orkney did indeed roost. Any iron or steel object, any equipment or tools left unprotected for a day, would start to roost, and anything that needed to be fixed either had roost problems, or the roost was the problem. When the hens were sleeping that was called roosting; when the hinges on the hen house door seized-up that was also called roosting. We always understood what each other meant. A 'rooster' was also a male hen or cockerel, but nothing was really as complicated as it all seemed.

Other construction that took place in and around the shed included a slide from the roof of the peat shed down to the green at the clothes-line. A see-saw, with a ships plank and the rest of the assembly, was modified every week, usually with a barrel, oil drum or some other ingenious wooden assembly. Our major permanent construction, however, was a swing made from heavy galvanised water pipes, with thirteen-foot high uprights set in concrete bases about six and half feet apart, with a cross-bar of the same size pipe as the uprights, all screw-jointed together. Two shackle hooks were fitted to this cross-bar/pipe, and we had the swing supports – two smaller diameter pipes down to a solid pipe link – which was fitted with a wooden seat. This swing was just as solid as the Churchill Barriers and proved indestructible, even by us.

Directly opposite this shed was the peat shed, built of ships' planks, with open spaces covered in galvanised wire-netting. This was where the peats were stacked and stored. I once had a hedgehog who used to live in here, and since the sides were relatively open it could get in and out at will. He was quite tame and never really travelled very far.

Alongside the peat shed was a tattie shed which was small and low like a garden hut. This was where the hens' food and tatties were kept. Next to the back door of the house, against the wall, we had a steel water-tank to collect the roof rainwater. This was supported on a steel structure approximately ten feet high which was enclosed to form another small hut with a door, which was only ever referred to as 'under the tank'. This hut was used to store ladders, spades, shovels, rakes, forks – all sorts of garden implements and other useful stuff.

Next to the peat shed was the clothes drying-green, a square of approximately thirty-three feet with a steel pole (pipe) at each corner, and a clothes-line wire connecting all four sides, along with a diagonal line for awkward winds. There were also wooden prop-poles for use if the washing was extra heavy.

At the bottom end of the property, next to the links border, we had a hen house. It was a very solid wooden structure which looked like what is now known as a Wendy House. It was also quite big, having an additional room with its own entrance and separate door at the back. The main hen-house section was well constructed with a lockable hinged door, windows on two sides, special nest boxes with straw for the hens to lay their eggs in, and perches at one end for them to roost on at night. Apparently hens sleep standing up on perches. Our hen population used to vary between fifteen and thirty birds, depending on how many were kept for laying eggs and how many got eaten. Although the hens were sometimes allowed to run free everywhere, they were usually confined inside a wire-mesh enclosure with direct access in and out of the hen house. Although this enclosure was about ten foot high, some of them still managed to fly over the top and escape. We had to resort to clipping the long feathers on one wing and that was them grounded for at least a month until the feathers grew again.

To increase our fowl population we always used one of our own hens to sit on a new batch of eggs – anything between nine and twelve eggs at a time. These eggs were either from our own production or, by some local exchange or other arrangement, from one of the neighbours' flocks. Although we had white, black and black-white hens, the majority were always shades of brown. We always had hens and seemed to have varying number of other fowl such as turkeys, geese, ducks, and even bantams which were just half-size hens anyway.

The standard hen food was oats and pellets, but we also fed them boiled mash made with corn, potato and other vegetable skins and peelings. Sometimes we gave them fish, and a few handfuls of maize meal and some special red Karswood Spice to stimulate egg production. For water my father had rigged up a drinking trough with the valve-and-float system out of an old toilet cistern. This worked perfectly, supplied as it was by their own hen-house roof rain-tank water supply by the gravity feed system. We also fed them special grit (necessary for good egg-shells, or the hen's digestive system – or both). This grit had to be just right and was specially collected from certain parts of the beach only. When we let the hens free every now and then from their prison enclosure, they would roam around and eat any-thing, especially earthworms and all sorts of other insects, not to mention the cat food.

Smokey the cat was always around when we came back from fishing, knowing there was always a few fish available. He was always first in the queue for food. Now the cats and hens, who always co-existed together with a sort of uneasy truce, knew that any fighting or all-out war was totally forbidden and would be dealt with accordingly. However, Smokey just couldn't resist a hen, especially when there were dozens of new day-old chicks running around just for the taking; he had to catch one or two, kill them and eat them. One time he got caught with the evidence and was instantly convicted and sentenced. When Smokey knew he was guilty, he never tried to run away; instead, he would crouch down and cower at your feet, hoping for a reprieve. But there would be no reprieve this time; it was up by the scruff of the neck and into the drum of water next to the shed to be held under for about five to six seconds. If the crime was really bad, this was repeated for another five seconds. The drookeled Smokey would then slink away and be on his best behaviour – for at least a week or two.

Whether the hens and other fowls were in or out of their official residence, the hen house and the food and water equipment all needed cleaning. This was our job – every Saturday – and always involved any two of us in no particular order. Since we got paid threepence each, we always did the job diligently and it never really seemed like hard work. I also think it made the hens happy, so it was worth all the effort. So, with shovels and hoes, we cleaned out the manure and then sprinkled clean dry sand on the relatively clean floor. Then we scraped all the perches, changed the straw in the nest boxes, and made sure each box had a 'nest egg'. This nest egg was a life-sized artificial porcelain egg, there to remind the hens that it was their job to lay an egg every day – and it seemed to work. Indeed, sometimes it worked so well that we even got the odd double-yolker egg. The manure and old straw were always put in the midden – for future use, as fertilizer for our flowers or vegetables.

Our mum, before she was married, used to work in a real job in nursing and homecare in mainland Scotland and, I think, even in London with her sister Molly. Now that she was married with all of us (and we were all born at home, hospitals were only for people who were ill or injured), her new job was a much bigger one, looking after us. Although we thought we helped sometimes, it was probably us that caused most of her work, and we usually only helped out if forced or bribed.

One of the jobs that I did help with, without being forced or bribed, was fowl procurement and processing. Every now and then, one of our livestock – usually a hen, turkey or goose – was specially selected to be sacrificed for the benefit of its keepers. My part, starting with discussion and selection, was the catch-and-kill phase. Although I treated all the livestock well, I did have my favourites. But once the decision was made, I treated the catch-and-kill as normal, routine stuff, without too much drama and emotion – although I might be a bit sad. Having arranged my Executioner's equipment – initially a steel rod – I then caught the approved victim, which was never too difficult, picked it up and took it to the designated place of dispatch – which was always discretely away from the general fowl tribe. Then, holding my victim up by its two legs in one hand, and with its head on the ground, I put my killer steel rod across its neck on the ground in front of me. Putting one foot on each end of the rod, thereby trapping the victim, I bent and pulled at the same time, breaking its neck – death was almost instantaneous.

I very rarely asked my brothers for assistance. Anyway, when it was their turn to do the deed, they didn't seem to want my help.

When I was about ten – and dealing with very big geese – my earlier dispatch system didn't work very well. On one or two occasions, my victims actually challenged me and had the audacity to fight back. Just so they fully understood who was in charge, I took my axe and, with one chop, cut their heads off. But as this wasn't considered the correct way of doing things, I mastered a more humane technique.

Next, I had to hang the quarry up by its feet behind the back door, and that was it until the next day when it was my job to do the plucking. All the big feathers went into one basket and all the small down-stuff into the other – this plucking took hours and it definitely wasn't my favourite job. Eventually, when it was finished, I think the feathers got used for something, like stuffing pillows or cushions. I experimented with making quill pens out of some of the big feathers and, when the nib was cut just right and dipped in the ink, they worked quite well. We even made flies for fishing with some of the feathers.

The night after the plucking or the next day, my mother took over. First of all she got a dustpan or shovel and methylated spirits. A quarter-cup of meths was poured into the shovel (outside on the step) and lit. The recently plucked fowl was now singed all over to remove small feathers and things that inadvertently I may have overlooked. We now had a perfect, completely bald fowl. While all this singeing and smell of burning was going on, the cats came out to investigate. Oddly enough, just by coming near and sniffing around – in these few minutes – made them totally intoxicated and they would roll around the floor helpless, apparently enjoying it, for about five minutes. I used to think this was really funny and tried to encourage it, especially with Smokey, until I got caught by my mother and had to pretend I was just doing my job and keeping the cats at a safe distance.

Once the fowl (and felines) had been dealt with, it was onto the slab. The slab was the kitchen sink right-hand side worktop, next to the pump. My job was as general factotum and observer. Strange as it may seem, even to me now, I quite looked forward to watching the proceedings. First Mum put on her pinny, which she always tied in a bow behind her back. This always amazed me, considering I had great difficulty tying a bow even while looking at it. Now the butchering really began.

Warning – the squeamish should stop reading here and go on to the next paragraph! For with a completely bald and cold fowl flat on its back, and usually complete with head, feet and wings, the head was cut off and placed into the white, enamelled basin in the sink. After the head came the neck, which we kept, so this was left on the slab. Next the quern or gizzard was taken out and the innards of half-digested oats and grit removed and put into the basin. All things discarded went into the basin, while the quern itself went onto the slab next to the neck. Now the other end was cut open and all the guts pulled out into the basin.

Sometimes, if we were lucky, there would be a soft-shelled egg here – a complete normal egg, but soft like rubber because it hadn't developed its hard shell yet. We kept the egg, quern and neck, that's all. Then the feet got chopped off at the drumstick and put into the basin. Finished, the hen's body was put into another basin of salt-water for a final clean and wash, ready for cooking. The basin of offal was then sorted out, some thrown out and some boiled up for cat food.

All this took about half an hour and although I never did it myself, I was always enthralled and never missed a stage.

If the prepared body was for roasting, it would be stuffed with a mixture of oatmeal and onions and spices – both ends – and actually sewn up before cooking. The quern and neck usually got boiled separately and used in the soup.

Now Mum always did the fowl and Dad always did the rabbits, but when it came to fish anyone could do them. I usually gutted my own, and cut their heads off. I would even fillet them, which I did for special occasions. All the fish processing was usually done outside, if not at the Barrier or beach before taking them home. However, filleting at home was always favourite with the cats, who ate everything raw straight from the sea – all this was just accepted as normal and natural.

The remainder of the ground around the house was made up of growing areas. Ian, Gavin and myself started off with our own personal gardens, each about thirty by fifteen feet. We initially grew all sorts of flowers, either from seeds or from neighbours' gardens or (our favourite) anything we saw growing wild that we could dig up and transplant. This all added up to a great mix of everything, including daffodils, tulips, hyacinths (blue, pink and white bells), snowdrops, crocuses, roses, lupins, red-hot pokers, marguerite daisies, pansies, night-scented stock and something called London Pride. There were also various other plants, bulbs and ground-cover, small bushes, white lilies, tiger lilies, nasturtiums and geraniums. While we grew flowers, which seemed to give us some enjoyment for a few years at least, our father grew vegetables such as potatoes, cabbages, cauliflowers, Brussels sprouts, shallots (onions), lettuce, carrots, beet-root, radishes, turnips, big butterbeans and peas – my favourite. Peas were by far the best. We ate them straight from the pod and sometimes they were so delicious that we ate the pod as well (my granny called the pods the slughs).

Somehow, no matter what we grew, weeds always grew much faster, and far better; no matter how much we pulled them out or hacked them down, they just kept on growing.

The other thing that grew almost as well as weeds was rhubarb which we would eat by sticking the ends into a paper poke of sugar – because rhubarb always tasted a little bit acidic. We had rhubarb jam, tarts and stewed rhubarb and custard. Rhubarb never seemed to come to an end.

When our father planted potatoes, he would dig a trench about a foot deep and put fertiliser all the way along the bottom. This fertiliser might be seaweed (which we carted from the beach), or compost (from the compost heap), or peat mould (direct from the peat bog), or the peat dust left in the peat shed, or chicken manure from the hen-house midden – or a mixture of all of this. This worked reasonably well, although the soil was very sandy – especially when compared to the really black earth ploughed by the farmers. Anyway, when the fertiliser was put in the trench (usually my job if I hadn't managed to scheme some special trip or errand to get out of such hard labour), the seed potatoes were planted, approximately eighteen inches apart. Sometimes the seed potatoes were cut in half, and as long as each half had eyes it would grow. This trench was filled in by digging the next parallel trench, and so on, and so on – until we had a huge area of potatoes planted.

Potatoes, of course, are not just potatoes and we seemed to have a variety of all sorts, shapes and sizes – Golden Wonders (white), Duke of York (white), Kerr's Pink (pink), Kidneys (purple) and Black Hearts. When cut in half, the Black Hearts looked a bit like kiwi fruit with a dark centre surrounded by a circle and lots of little dots.

The other vegetables were easier to plant in rows from seed, but they still needed thinning out or transplanting when they got bigger, and there were always the weeds to sort out. Another problem was insects – especially worms – that always got to the carrots and neeps before we did. However, with ingenious concoctions of D.D.T. and other stuff, we kept the bugs reasonably under control.

We also grew strawberries and the greatest success of this was achieved by Ian when he took barrowloads of soft peat straight out the bog, making a level bed of this without mixing it into the ground, and planted his strawberries in it. This resulted in the best strawberries ever, year after year.

Life seemed to run fairly routinely until I was seven or eight, when circumstances seemed to change. Our baby brother Colin was now four years of age and I was no longer the youngest. Ian and Ruthie had now left our Burray School and gone to high school, and I had just got my first bike.

So as this new phase of my life began, I was still living with my mother, father, two brothers older than me and a younger brother, and an independent granny, Mary Bruce (my mother's mother). I never ever saw either of my two grandfathers or my other grandmother, even though I'm sure Alexander MacKenzie – my father's father, a retired station-master in Crianlarich on mainland Scotland – only died when I was five or six.

My mother was often assisted by Jesse Wylie or Betty Scott, who were friends and some sort of 'home-help' people. On a typical Saturday during summer, I would get up early at seven and dress myself in simmit, pants, shirt, jeans or dungarees, two pairs of socks, jersey, zip-up jerkin, welly-boots – but no gloves or hat. I then washed hands and face with Lifebuoy soap – no shower, no bath – and brushed my teeth with Gibbs teeth cleaner (a round cake-like soap in a flat tin). We always used Cold Tar shampoo for our hair. Usually I made my own breakfast of boiled egg or fried, then I would sprinkle parsley or shallot tops on it. Sometimes it would be porridge (made with the famous, traditional Scott's Porridge Oats) and tea (never coffee), toast, marmalade and rhubarb jam (both homemade).

If I was first up, or if everyone else had no time, I would clean out the fire. All the ashes went into the special ash bucket to be dumped when full. However, any cinders or other unburnt stuff went back into the fire, along with rolled-up pages from the *The Orcadian*, kindling sticks – which if you were lucky someone had left in the oven from the night before – and then some coal on top, and a dash of paraffin. Strike a match and that was the fire going, which then needed continuous feeding of logs, coal or peats for the rest of the day. When Granny lit the fire, she never used paraffin, but a spoonful of sugar or candlewax instead. And when she cleaned up the floor around the fireplace, as I recall, she moved a floor cloth around with her foot – which I have never seen anyone do before or since.

I would then take the garden rake and a bucket, and with one of my brothers, though sometimes alone, we'd go down to the beach – over three hundred yards walk at low tide – and rake in the sand and get dozens of cockles (clams) for fish-bait. We would also catch small crabs, sand eels, sand shrimps, huge lug worms and mussels and limpets off the rocks and sometimes pick up live purple sea-urchins as big as Jaffa oranges – with hundreds of spikes. We never harmed them and they were always left to go free.

At low tide we put out a long net to catch fish, with lead weights along the bottom, cork floats along the top and very heavy, iron anchor weights at both ends. The idea was, when the tide came in, the fish would get caught in the net and we would collect our spoils at low tide. Although this resulted in a few flounders, and even a sea trout once, it wasn't one of our most successful endeavours. However, wading out into the sea, preferably at low tide, I would track and spear flounders with my own home-made spear – a galvanised six-inch nail flattened and filed into an arrow-head and stuck into the end of a rake handle. My all time record was three flounders in one day.

So having collected the cockles and other bait, and as the tide came in between noon and six in the evening, we would take our rods and go fishing. This was usually at the pier in the village if it was during the day before six, but from six until midnight we always went to the Barrier. Fishing was about great fun and excitement, but it was also very serious stuff.

Inside Scapa Flow, at our swimming beach, we always found jellyfish sitting on the beach at low tide. This beach had the big six-inch to two-foot in diameter brown-red jellyfish, whereas on the outside of the barrier, on the *Carron** side, there were always the smaller four- to twelve-inch blue translucent type. Strangely enough, the small blues usually got left alone.

Because we had heard that jellyfish can sting you (although I don't think we ever got stung), but anyway, just in case, we deployed pre-emptive measures when we found the big brown ones sitting on our swimming beach. This might entail whoever was there at the time taking dozens of stones and smashing the fierce and deadly creatures to smithereens. This wasn't really full-scale slaughter, I hasten to add, because sometimes we slid them onto a wooden plank or board and launched them into the sea to find out how they swim, or indeed if they could swim. They always did and I think they avoided coming back as much as possible.

Even when we were fishing, we would see them swimming around – we didn't bother them and they didn't bother us.

Another creature that sat on the beach when the tide went out was the comper, a sort of puffer fish, apparently poisonous. They just sat on the beach sand and we would pick them up carefully since they had a huge mouth and spikes everywhere. Sometimes we stuck small corks onto the spikes on their sides and on their heads and put them back in the water to watch them trying to swim around and dive, but we always removed the corks in the end and let them go unharmed.

The other creatures that got caught at low tide were scallops. Although not plentiful, and usually not much bigger than the palm of your hand, these scallops were delicious grilled with butter.

---

*H.M.S. *Carron* was a block-ship, sunk in Scapa Flow in March 1940.

Daytime fishing – usually in the hot sun – only involved catching small-fry, but sometimes we came across a shoal of mackerel. This fish would bite at anything and, though they were strong and always put up a fight, they were quite easy to hook. However, they always swept past very quickly and we could only catch one or two before the shoal was gone. The Barrier fishing was definitely better – with the possibility of big fish and big catches – which did happen now and again, with one or two reasonably sized cod, weighing up to five pounds. Sometimes we even caught a three-foot-long dogfish, which we either killed or threw back into the sea, depending on how badly hooked it was. Our main catches were saithe, pollock, wrasse, flounder and the non-edible compers.

We sometimes saw huge conger eels up to twelve feet long, but we never tried to catch them. Even bigger creatures swimming around included basking sharks up to thirty feet in length, and white beluga whales of ten to twelve feet (which always looked too small for being a whale!). Now and again some sea creature would get washed up on the shore and this was always of great interest. One day an orca, a black and white killer whale – really a dolphin – got washed up ashore, dead – or at least it was dead when we found it. Ian wanted some souvenir orca teeth and used his pocket knife to remove a few – I think he still has them to this day.

During our fishing adventures we were often bothered by seals, otters and even cormorants trying to get in on the action. This, of course, frightened the fish away. Since our competition refused to shift, it was easier for us to move further along the Barrier or over to the opposite side to get completely away from them.

From the age of about eight, and having a bike, I was into money-making schemes along with my brothers. One of these ventures – which made almost no money at all – was to catch fish and give them away to neighbours, based on the assumption that if they accepted the fish they would give us a few shillings or whatever they thought was a reasonable exchange.

To them, however, it seemed more reasonable to accept the fish and give us nothing.

The venture that did make money was whelk-gathering. With Ian, Gavin, and sometimes a friend, like Alfie Tait, we all went down to the rocks on the beach at low tide and simply picked the whelks off the rocks and put them in a bucket. When the bucket was full, we poured its contents into a communal sack. On good days at really low tides, we managed to get a reasonable quota to sell. This had to be at least a bushel, which was half a sack, the maximum we could handle and transport. If we got less before the tide turned, we would find a secret safe place in the rocks and tie the jute sack and put a few stones on top, and then we left it there until the next day at low tide. We always managed our quota of one to three bushels over two days.

We somehow managed our own quality-control about size and purity – no stones, seaweed or other creatures – although this always created some heated discussions and arguments, but the job went on regardless until the tide came in and we made off with our hard-earned catch. That was the first stage of the job.

The next stage involved getting the whelks home from the beach by carrying a bagful of them from the rocks to the road – three hundred or so yards – to our bikes. Transporting the whelks home by bike could be done in a couple of ways: one was to put a bag of whelks onto the carrier behind the seat, although it was usually too heavy and awkward to handle. The other way was, if we had a really good catch, to put the sack over the cross-bar and walk home.

Since all this happened at the weekend, once the whelks were brought back, we selected the best jute sack available and filled it to the maximum – or put half-and-half in two sacks if there were too many whelks. We then tied a metal label onto the securely-sealed sacks with 'to' and 'from' names and addresses. The 'to' was always D. Miel & Sons, Kirkwall, approximately fourteen miles away by road, on the main island. Of course we also kept some for ourselves, and would boil a big potful and sit around the table at home, eating them straight out of their shells with safety pins.

Although Kirkwall has always been the capital town of Orkney, the main island used to be called Pomona. This was later changed by a committee of geniuses, no doubt after months of deliberation, and they came up with the extremely original name of Mainland, even though the real mainland of Scotland is less than twenty miles south, across the sea. However, I digress.

The next stage was to transport the whelks by road, from home to Kirkwall. This was always done by the D. Spence & Sons bus service. Although there were three or four different bus drivers on this route, by far the slowest was Jack Walls. When told once by an irate passenger that he could get out and walk quicker, Jack, quick as a flash, retorted, so could he but he had to take the bus with him and that the extra weight slowed him down. Nonetheless, it was a good reliable bus service and it departed from St Margaret's Hope in South Ronaldsay at seven in the morning – three miles away. It eventually got to us after all its various stops at round about quarter past seven.

The bus stopped for passengers and freight anywhere along the route and it was multi-purpose – passengers, school kids, freight and anything else that you could get onto a bus, which was a modern single-decker seating about forty folk. When the bus stopped, the driver got out – there wasn't a conductor – and opened the boot. We then loaded our sacks of whelks and off he went. There was never any conversation.

The whelks were received, checked, measured, weighed and paid for by D. Miel & Sons – ten shillings a bushel.

Along with the whelk enterprise, we caught and sold lobsters and spoots, which were razor clams. Like the whelks, both activities were during the 'r' months – September to April, from autumn through winter until spring, which of course were the coldest months. This 'r' in the month way of doing things came about because this was when it was acceptable to gather most sea creatures – out of the breeding season. Anyway, catching spoots from a bystander's point of view appeared very easy, but in practice it was not so. First of all, the very low spring tides were best, and the colder the better, with snow and ice on the ground and freezing temperatures being the absolutely ideal. It worked best with a very low tide on a sandy beach, and only then if it was a good spoot beach – usually with fine-grained, hard sand. We had two good spoot beaches – one at the village pier (my favourite), and the other at Etna Loch, one and a quarter miles away by bike. So, we'd go down to the beach at the pier, at very low tide, freezing cold, wearing as many layers of clothes as possible, at least two of everything, and welly-boots.

You had to get as close to the edge of the sea as possible, and all this in competition with the old fogey experts around you. Choosing your position, you then walked slowly backwards. The reason for walking backwards was that spoots had dug themselves into the sand, just level or slightly under the surface, and when you walked over the sand they would shoot out a spoot of water and tunnel down several feet very quickly. If you were walking forwards as normal, all this was happening behind you and you were completely unaware of it. So by walking backwards, the instant the spoot activated you were onto it.

The 'onto it' worked like this. You had your spoot-hunting equipment in your hand at the ready. This consisted of a large-bladed knife (not sharp) and perhaps a small digging spade or trowel (optional). If you were a really good spoot hunter, which of course I imagined I was, then you didn't need the digger tool. So walking backwards, the spoot activated, you knew where it was (it also knew where you were), and in less than a split nanosecond, with your knife, you stuck into the sand, aiming for approximately the middle of the vertical side of your prey. The average spoot was about eight inches long, like a half-squashed pipe, with an oval cross-section of about an inch and hinged down one of its long sides. The two sides were two separate razor shells which opened and closed opposite the hinged side. Having scored a direct hit, you then pinned the spoot against the side of the escape tunnel, and with your other hand grabbed your prey before it could move. Then with great dexterity, you yanked the spoot out of the sand before it could retaliate and counter your attack by digging itself in further and escaping. If you missed with your first strike, or were too slow, it was tedious and difficult to dig down to capture your prey, so you moved on to your next unsuspecting victim.

All this activity took place within a limited time before the tide turned, usually a maximum of one hour, and only a few days in any month. At really low tides, and in really freezing conditions with ice and snow on the ground, the spoots would stick up half out of the sand by themselves and you could creep up and pick them up without walking backwards. This was so rare, however, I think I saw it only twice in my life. I would say that on a good hunting day twenty spoots was a fair catch, with fifty an all-time record.

The spoots were good to eat if put straight into boiling water (to make them instantly open out of their shells) and then fried in butter – same-day, fresh from the sea. They were similar in texture to calamari, but much tastier.

After two or three days of spoot-hunting, and keeping them alive in the sea, a hundred spoots would be carefully placed into a tailor-made wooden box with some seaweed for packing, with a hinged lid and a hasp-closing system. They were then labelled and shipped off as usual to D. Miel & Sons, Kirkwall. This always resulted in an immediate money-order payment of £2.10/-, being the going rate of sixpence a spoot.

Our lobster enterprise was perhaps more difficult. Local crofters and fishermen would launch their motor boats, loaded up with eight to ten creels baited with half a mackerel or other fish heads (usually pickled in brine from the previous season). The creels were then dropped in the best lobster and partan locations and left overnight. Each individual creel had a rope attached, with cork floats at three-foot intervals and a plastic or aluminium buoy at the end – as the master float and marker. The next day the creels would be pulled up one at a time. Any lobsters, partans, or sometimes fish and other sea creatures, would be removed, and any undersized or unwanted ones returned to the sea. The process would then be repeated, and the creels re-launched or redistributed, depending on how good the catch was. My own endeavours were not that great. Although I made creels and placed them strategically amongst the rocks at low tide, and even launched them over the side of the Barriers, neither system was particularly successful.

I eventually devised a more direct approach, which again meant going down to the beach – a different beach – at low tide on my bike. This was across the Barrier, another five hundred and fifty yards along the road in South Ronaldsay. This beach, although sandy at low tide, had huge rocks and rockpools and so my attempt at lobster-hunting involved looking for rocks with sand tunnels burrowed under them.

Once a likely lobster lair was located, I deployed my special lobster-hunting tools – a steel L-shaped bar, about three-foot long, with a leg-hook end. This was in fact the back bar of a grass-cutting scythe-blade of the grim reaper variety – perfect for lobster hunting.

Having traced the creature to its lair, I ventured in with the hook-end. If the lobster was at home, it would immediately go on the defensive or try to escape. If the rock was in a sea-pool, it would often make a dash for the water and swim off. Now although lobsters crawl around forward – looking at you with their two big claws at the ready in front – they actually swim backwards. So when you are chasing them, you still have the claws facing you. I have heard that lobsters can reach swimming speeds of up to thirty miles an hour! However, these rockpools were not big enough to reach such acceleration – the water was barely knee-deep, and the pools not very big. No wonder then that after a few minutes of hunt and escape, I would eventually corner my prey and catch it – without it catching me.

A lobster weighing five to six pounds, is very agile and fierce, with huge claws that have been known to inflict serious damage on a would-be captor. Fortunately, this never happened to me. At ten or eleven years of age at the time, although I never wore gloves, it was probably more or less a fair fight. And so, to catch one lobster at each low tide was not unusual.

Now a lobster can live out of water for quite some time, at least a day or two, so it was home with the catch – after tying its claws closed to prevent any problems – and into the holding tank. This was a large zinc bath which got a change of sea-water twice a week and had all the standard amenities of sand, rocks, seaweed, shells, and even some small live creatures. The next day the lobsters would be packed into a special wooden lobster box with fresh seaweed and shipped off to D. Miel & Sons. A lobster was priced according to size and weight, but it always seemed to work out at approximately £5 each. When you are ten, this is a good deal.

Lobsters are great to eat straight from the sea and boiled. Although dark blue-black in colour, they turn bright red when cooked.

There were other enterprises that we started which didn't prove to be quite so lucrative, although they did entail a great deal of hard work. I think the worst of all was 'the peats'. Now peats are peats, and looking back, I believe people actually imagined a little thatched-roofed crofter's cottage in the middle of winter, with Mr and Mrs McCrofter sitting on their rocking chairs, with the two bairns huddled up next to them, all dressed in tartan and cosy in front of a roaring peat fire. Then there is what really happened.

The peat bog was approximately half a mile from where we lived. It was not a wet swamp, but a marshy wasteland that could not be used for arable farming. Our fresh water Eel Burn, which ran out of Etna Loch and the Lye Well, ran all the way through this peat bog. Digging the peats worked like this. My father, with only a spade, would clear the top growth of grass, heather and moss, and the topsoil, to a depth of about two feet to uncover the actual peat bank. Peat is actually trees and other vegetation from thousands of years previous which have decayed into a semi-pulp texture, similar in consistency to a mature cheese, although there can be actual tree trunks and branches which are equally as soft to cut and dig. The peats were cut and dug out by my father, each about the size of a box of washing-powder or cornflakes and, when wet, each one weighed about two pounds.

When Dad had dug out the peats, he placed them on the bank of the peat quarry, then the three of us picked them up, one at a time, and would lay them out flat on the grass, near to the peat diggings at first. Naturally, the more we laid them out, the further we had to walk. We devised various schemes to try to beat the system, however the result was always the same – the longer you worked, the further you had to carry the peats, the more tired you got. This seemed to go on forever, although it was probably about four hours on any one day, resulting in the production of about four hundred peats.

Having completed this batch, we waited for two to three days before returning to the laid-out peats. They were now half-dry and a bit more durable. Since this was all done during the summer, nature worked with us when we turned them over to dry on the other side. Approximately a week later, the peats were stacked in a four-sided pyramid, with one peat flat on top. Soon there were thousands of peats all over the place.

The peat, when dug out of the bog, was noted for having nothing living in it. There were worms, ants and other insects in the top soil, but nothing lived in the actual peat material. There was also no stones, and it hardly had any noticeable smell (not until it was burned, anyway).

Now, we were not the only boys involved in this peat production – or in the collection of the huge mushrooms which would spring up near the peat in clusters overnight, especially after rain. These mushrooms were as big as dinner-plates or as small as golf-balls, and though toadstools were just as plentiful, we always knew exactly which were edible and which were poisonous. The mushrooms were delicious when peeled and fried in butter.

When we were there with the other boys, and without our father, the peat or mushroom collecting often descended into a peat fight with tennis-ball-sized hard or soft clumps being thrown at each other. These ferocious fights took place between two parallel barbed-wire fences, about sixty or so feet apart, which constituted quite a hazard, especially when we got trapped by the enemy and ran out of ammunition. I still have some barbed-wire scars for souvenirs.

Apart from mushrooms, we also collected wild blackberries and blueberries from the heather which we put into jam jars. If there were too many to eat there and then, we took several jars home to our mother to make really good blackberry jam.

When the peats were declared ready and fully-matured, they were put into jute sacks and loaded onto a wheel barrow and pushed the roughly two-thirds of a mile home. This sometimes continued all day Saturday and seemed like never-ending labour – which it was. Once home, the peats were stacked and packed into the peat shed.

The peat was used at home for fire fuel and they burned with a blue smoke and haze. But they did burn well, when eventually you got them going, and the glow and heat was really quite nice.

* * *

Insects seemed to be involved in my life for as long as I can remember, and Orkney never seemed to run out of varieties – and then endless numbers of each. We had bumblebees, which I used to pick off wild flowers and capture in jam jars. The bees were mainly two types – black and yellow as well as brown. Apparently they could sting, but I didn't know this and anyway they never stung me. After catching a jarful, I would take them home, open the lid and let them free again.

There were also butterflies – Red Admirals, blue types and the common White Cabbage butterfly. Moths, flies and bluebottles were also never in short supply and every now and again we got swarms of midges, although never any mosquitoes. We got wasps and horseflies and clegs, which would settle on you and sting if you didn't get them first. There were also ants, slaters, centipedes and all sorts of black and brown beetles, and a thing that looked a bit like a scorpion, without claws, that was jet black. Scaly and up to about three inches long, this 'scorpion' lived under stones and wood and anything else that was lying around. Although they never caused us much trouble, we also didn't like to cause them much trouble either. My granny once told me that if you buried a dead mackerel, that it would turn into hundreds of these things – which she called 'black cloaks'. I never, ever tried to prove this – just in case it was true. Having even one around was one too many, and it did put me off eating mackerel for a few years – which was no big deal since we only ever really used them for bait to catch other fish.

We also had all kinds of spiders and flying daddy long-legs and grasshoppers or jumpers and various sorts of caterpillars and 'woolly bears' (hairy caterpillars). Our two main types of snails were bright yellow, and there was an enormous black slug which was almost as big as a mouse.

When we dug in the ground, we always found the usual earthworms, which we regarded as good and useful, but we also got wire worms and chaffer grubs which were bad and harmful. When we had a lot of these around, we used the hens as an efficient and environmentally-friendly insect control system and this also meant that I could keep my D.D.T. reserves for real emergencies.

The beasts that did cause constant annoyance were earwigs. They were everywhere, in spite of my all-out campaigns to have them totally eradicated. They got into the hen food, although I think the hens preferred eating them to their usual food. They also got into air vents, onto the walls, and even onto your clothes, and they were always on the peats. I don't know about anyone else, but I never made any attempt at getting them off the peats.

In the burn, loch and quarry, we spotted water beetles and boatmen; unless we tried to catch them, they didn't bother us much. At the beach, however, the only bugs seemed to be sea-slaters, seaweed jumpers (a sort of sea cricket) and thousands of fish moths or silverfish (which I think is the same thing). Although they swarmed around the rocks and barriers, as long as they stayed there that was fine.

With all this wildlife around us, one of the most exciting ventures for us at the time was finding birds' nests with eggs in them, and even with chicks that had just recently hatched. As I recall, we did have a reasonable code of honour, and by the time I was eleven I had become an official member of the Scottish SPCA, and the oath 'to be kind to all living creatures', and was given my certificate dated '1.8.1960' and signed in Edinburgh. Prior to this pledge, however, we did try to collect one egg from each type of bird to identify the species. This involved collecting, and then 'blowing' the egg – by making a hole in each end and blowing out the egg contents. This egg-hunting meant every-thing from tree and bush birds to ground-nesting birds, rock and cliff birds, and even swans (although we knew they were officially protected as royal game). All the eggs were carefully labelled, and packed with cotton wool in special cardboard boxes. Although our collection included sparrow, robin, thrush, starling, pigeon, plover, duck and water hens, the main prize was the swan's egg.

Getting a swan's egg was seriously dangerous stuff. With a huge nest built at the edge of the loch, it meant wading knee-deep through water and marsh. The two swans, male and female, were generally not too friendly when you were interfering with their offspring, and one was always on guard while the other was out hunting. When you are only seven or eight years old, a swan is as big as you, and if the swan was at home we had to abandon the mission.

It was exciting, but highly dangerous, to be climbing over the edge of cliffs, towering above the sea, dangling on the end of a rope to collect seagull, puffin and razorbill eggs. The seagulls and puffins were most unfriendly. To ensure there were no mis-haps, we devised our own methods of testing the ropes we used. This involved tying one end of the rope to a telegraph pole, and the three of us pulling on the other end. If the rope didn't break, it was given an official stamp of approval. Then, having complied with all our highly scientific and rigorous safety standards, we were ready.

The mission was simple – with one of us (i.e. me) dangling over the edge of the cliff, all the other two had to do was raise and lower according to instructions. So in spite of the noise from the crashing waves, the howling wind and the screaming sea birds, this seemed to have worked and through sheer luck, we (me) never ended up half-way down the cliff face – or worse, with a broken rope.

One of our favourite cliffs was on the east side of South Ronaldsay, not very far across the Barrier from Burray, about two miles from home. Although the rock cliffs were amazing, there were also walkways down to the sea, and one sort of walkway trench that ran along the side of the cliff close to the water that was always referred to as the Giant's Causeway. We were sure that some of the indentations in the rocks were definitely giant footprints, about three feet long, and made when the rocks were soft mud thousands of years before.

Although we collected wild birds' eggs, we did do some good in return. We had a black oystercatcher with a bright orange beak around for some time with an injured wing. After two or three months he recovered and was taken back to the beach to rejoin his family quite happily. A crow also came to stay when it was very small – just out of the nest – but eventually it became too big and started to eat everything. I even had to hunt rats and mice with my slug gun to keep it going. When the crow fought with the cats, it was finally sent back to the cliffs with all the other crows – and it never returned.

Percy the pigeon became a permanent resident after being taken from his nest in one of the shipwrecks and hand-reared with oatmeal, water and milk. Percy was a standard blue-black rock pigeon and he seemed to get on quite well with the tame white pigeons that Gavin kept. In fact he became too tame for his own good, as was proved one day when he flew down to eat the cats' food. The cats didn't approve and a fight broke out, with Percy losing several toes from one foot. He did eventually recover, but he never went near the cats again.

Percy liked to sit on my shoulder on the way to school, and would sometimes sit on the school roof, waiting for me to take him home.

*　　*　　*

The island of Hunda – Bird Island – is really a *sub*-island of Burray, about two-thirds of a mile by half a mile and sort of oval-shaped. It is on the west side of Burray, inside Scapa Flow, and linked to Burray by another causeway approximately a third of a mile long. This causeway had nothing whatsoever to do with the famous Churchill Barriers, and it could even have been there before them. Built by the locals, it is a considerable construction of huge rocks and stones in a dead-straight line, with a reasonable single lane on top. It's still used to this day – mainly by the farmers and probably risked by some tourists in their hired cars now and again, although at a very low tide it is just possible to walk on the sand all the way along the causeway. However, some very high tides cover the road completely. Since we knew all this, we never got marooned or stuck on Hunda.

When coming off the causeway onto Hunda, there is an old stone ruin (which I was told was once a kippering works) and some cottages, long-derelict and desolate even before my time. We did our bird observation and egg-collecting there. Hunda was almost completely covered in heather, with very little grass and, of course, no trees – a sort of birds' paradise – even with us there. Various sea-birds would swoop down and attack us, especially if we got too near their nests. There were also sparrowhawks and a few owls as well. When we collected the big eider blue duck eggs – which we called a 'dunter' duck – we tried not to waste the eggs and would usually feed it to the cats. We also learned or got told that if you took two or three of these eggs – there were sometimes as many as nine in a nest – you could make a really nice omelette with them. So we did and agreed this was true.

Animals, wild and tame, were always plentiful on the island, and they came in all shapes and sizes. We always had cats, a minimum of two going up to six. Other animals came and went, including a hedgehog which we dug out of its hibernation burrow in the sand quarry. We then went on to do it a great favour by keeping it as a pet. Although we fed it, it was free to roam and find what it wanted for itself.

White rabbits, anything from two to four, were also kept in a hutch with a wire-mesh run. Now, although we hunted wild rabbits, tame white rabbits were different. The run was moved around on the grass once or twice a week, so that the rabbits could have new grass, clover and any other vegetation that happened to be growing there. This also prevented them from having enough time in one place to burrow under the edge of the run and escape. However, we still had to feed them and give them water. Their favourite food was clover – with red or white flowers – and dandelions, both the leaves and the bright yellow flowers. Since rabbits are strict vegetarians, we also gave them carrots, neeps, cabbage and lettuce leaves.

Two guinea-pigs were also residents, though not for too long; despite being in a hutch and run, the cats somehow managed to get in and kill both of them. The chief suspect was Smokey the fighting cat – as usual. Although I had the two bodies, I never managed to get sufficient evidence (this time) to convict Smokey, which let him off the hook again – for a short time at least. I conducted the funeral.

We always seemed to keep one or two goldfish in a bowl on the sideboard. Not a sophisticated aquarium, just a goldfish bowl with sand and a few rocks. We fed them with ants' eggs and changed the water about twice a week. Since goldfish were fairly easy to keep, I decided to experiment with frogs and toads. I went down to one of the ponds and searched around amongst the water weeds at the edge until I found where the frogs, tadpoles and frogspawn were. Armed with my bucket and glass jar, I captured a few dozen eggs which were taken home and placed in a glass bowl with water and marsh weeds, and all set up on a table in the boiler house. After a few days the eggs got bigger, and after about a week I had a few tadpoles swimming around. The next day there were dozens, some with tails, others with hind legs.

Now everyone knows that tadpoles and frogs live in water, but no one told me that once the tadpoles turn into frogs, they have to get out of the water onto dry land now and again, to breathe. My lack of knowledge on amphibious matters resulted in half my frogs drowning.

I came up with an emergency frog rescue plan, which involved pouring out half the water, adding some rocks and supplying them with small pieces of wood as sort of rescue boats. This worked fine until the amphibians were about the size of my hand and getting bigger by the minute. I now had to do something fast. This involved capturing and containing twenty leaping amphibians and getting them into a bucket and back to their original habitat.

They seemed pleased to be returned home and all dived in and swam as deep and as far away from me as possible. Although I often looked around for them during the days that followed, they were obviously so glad to escape that they kept well out of sight.

Other wildlife which I remember were the wild rabbits, hares, rats, mice and shrews on dry land, and otters and seals on the beach and in the sea.

* * *

School was strictly attended every day, Monday to Friday, unless you were seriously ill, and no matter what the weather was. Burray School was a very nice stone building with a slate roof, wooden doors and wooden sash windows which opened by sliding up and down. The school was made up of three main sections. The first, where we all started off, was called the lower end. The last, from where we graduated to the high school, was called the upper end. The mid-section was, naturally, called the middle end, and that was it. The lower end had girls' and boys' porches, and outside was the boys' toilet. The upper end had a communal porch and the girls' toilets were round the back. The school grounds were completely surrounded by a stone wall, with a big wooden gate. The playground, which was really just stony earth and sand, was eventually flattened and completely covered by tarmacadam about two years before I left.

The lower end was built on a sloping wooden floor so that we all looked down towards the teacher (Mrs Lilian Gray), the blackboard, and the fireplace. The anthracite coal fire was nearly always on and, even in the middle of winter, despite the ice and snow, it kept the place quite warm. The big, round Roman numeral clock was affixed to the same wall, to the side of the fireplace. The desks were in rows, each one a two-seater unit made of solid wood, with a hinged-top and a cast-iron frame bolted to the floor. The upper end had individual and more modern, steel and wooden hinged-top desks; these were not fixed to the floor so that they could be moved around and rearranged to suit.

We sat in pairs and each class, of which I think there was three in this lower end, was divided into blocks from left to right facing the teacher.

Here it was that we started off learning all the basics – the three R's – reading, writing, arithmetic – as well as history and geography.

We were supplied with a half-pint bottle of milk each day – this seemed to be standard council or government procedure – and it was the boys' job to lug in the crate in every day, one for the lower end and one for the upper end. We took turns doing this.

At first, when we started school in year one, we were given slates and slate pencils to write on, but chalk was much better than slate pencils and soon became more popular. Later on we

1.

2.

3.

FIG. 1

Burray as viewed from the top of Big Brae. The Big Brae runs down to a T-junction. The Lye Well, Eel Burn and peat area is in the low area before the houses on the right

(*Copyright for all images:* Duncan Cameron Mackenzie)

FIG. 2

Duncan (middle) with his brothers Gavin (left) and Ian (right), 1950.

FIG. 3

Duncan (middle) with his brothers Gavin (left) and Ian (right), 1952.

4.

FIG. 4

Duncan (right) and his brother Gavin (left) on the roof of the house at Burray.

FIG. 5

Duncan (front) and friends paddling in the sea at Scapa Flow, Burray with Barrier No. 4 in the background.

5.

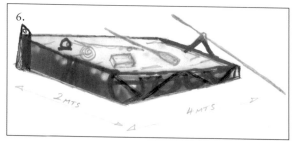

FIG. 6

Drawing of the raft constructed
and used by Duncan and friends.

FIG. 7

Drawing of a 'Neepie Lantern'
by Duncan Mackenzie.

FIG. 8

Duncan (front row, fourth from
left) with school classmates, 1954.

FIG. 9

Duncan (back row, right) with school classmates, 1956.

FIG. 10

Old Burray School,
Duncan's first school.

FIG. 11

Doull's grocery van at
Burray scrap-yard.

FIG. 12

Left to right – Gavin, Ian and
Duncan Mackenzie, 1956.

FIG. 13

Duncan (second from left) with
brothers Colin, Ian and Gavin,
with their cousin Nancy (left) and
Vera McDonald (right).

FIG. 14

'Gowan Braes', Duncan's
granny's house. Left to right –
Norman and Tommy (Duncan's
uncles), and Duncan's mother,
a neighbour and Granny.

FIG. 15

Duncan's granny, aged
approximately 70 years.

FIG. 16

The Lye Burn ditch from where
Duncan's family used to cut peats.
The peat-digging area is fenced on
each side by barbed wire.

FIG. 17

Burray village
from the top of
School Brae
looking towards
South Ronaldsay.

FIG. 18

Burray looking
towards South
Ronaldsay at
Barrier No. 4.

FIG. 19

People fishing on
Warebanks
Barrier No 3.

FIG. 20

Duncan with crane
engineering colleagues,
South Africa *c*.1992

FIG. 21

Duncan (back row,
sixth from left) at work-place
social event, 1994.

used jotters and lead pencils and rubbers. We even got real ink in our porcelain inkwells and had to fit new nibs into our ink pens. As I recall, the only way a new pen nib would hold the ink was if you licked it before putting it into the inkwell.

The teacher usually used white chalk on the blackboard, but sometimes used other colours to emphasise things better. We usually had to clean the blackboard with the duster and, on special occasions, were even allowed to write on it.

The upper end was where we finished Burray School, with Mr William Dickson sitting at his light-blue painted table on a horse-hair padded chair, usually with the tawse lurking in the table drawer. The hand-held bell always stood on the window and announced return to class time and the start of school each morning. Thirty seconds late almost certainly meant the tawse, even if it was a only first offence.

The middle end was where we had what passed for a library – a few bookshelves, with a few hundred books. There were also sinks and tables in this room, and when we got trainee teachers they would teach us art painting here. They also taught the girls Domestic Science – cooking, baking, knitting and sewing. We all liked going to the middle end, but this never seemed to happen very often. We also got music lessons, which usually involved the music teacher playing the piano and us all singing – although I did get to play the side drum in a school concert once. The school doctor, Dr Brodie, and nurse used to come to the school once or twice a year to check on us and give us our mandatory inoculations for the latest ailment going, for diseases like whooping cough, measles or chicken-pox.

Sport and play always existed at school, and we had all kinds of physical training and game events. Sport events were many and varied and included football, cricket, rounders, baseball, tug-of-war, running, relay race, long jump, high jump, sack race, egg-and-spoon race, three-legged race, leap frog, skipping and, a special event after school, swimming. During the year, a sort of ongoing training went, culminating in the main annual School Sports and picnic event, for Burray and South Ronaldsay combined. This was always held at St Margaret's Hope School. This was a major highlight, something we all looked forward to.

The Burray school daily/weekly sports always included rounders/baseball. This was really an official sport and was taken very seriously – and only the boys played. At the start of each month, two teams were established by having a captain in each team pick the players. This was all done on a fair and equitable basis. First of all, the two captains were chosen, and this choice was based mainly on some sort of rotation basis. Having established the two captains for the month, a coin was tossed and the winner got to choose the team name – either North or South – and get first pick of the players. This picking and choosing of players alternated between the two captains until all the available players were selected, ending up with between eight and twelve players for each team. It didn't matter if one team had nine players and the other had ten, because it was played on a time basis of two thirty-minute periods per week.

The final scores at the end of the sessions were recorded and added up until the month end. Then the four weekly scores were added up and the winning team announced. The prize for winning was a quarter-pound of Mackintosh's Quality Street, at one shilling per quarter pound – or so I thought. The tradition was that William Dickson, the headmaster, would give the captain of the winning team the money to buy each team member a quarter pound of Quality Street chocolates from the village shop.

This all seemed to work fine until the time I came to be captain and we won. In great excitement, I duly went to collect the prize – that was for nine plus myself, making ten packs of Quality Street. Having been given a pound note by Dickson, I bought the sweets and returned with them, and the change from the pound which was nine shillings and tuppence. Unbeknown to me, Quality Street had just gone up in price from a shilling a quarter pound to a shilling and a penny, for the first time in about two years. And therefore, on handing over the prize and change to the headmaster, he demanded to know why he wasn't given ten shillings change from his pound note. I explained that the Quality Street had gone up in price. But this was not acceptable, because apparently in his long-standing version of the rules, each player in the winning team got a prize of one shilling. However, it was understood by most of us that the sweets – and not the shilling – was the prize. Anyway after a lengthy and heated debate my team and I were eventually awarded our Quality Street prize.

The controversy raged on all during the next month until it came to prize-giving time again. Either through some consensus or a commonsense decision, the new rules were announced. From now on, the prize would be a quarter pound of Mackintosh's Quality Street per player in the winning team, irrespective of price – and I think the price stayed at a shilling and a penny until I left the school, (in 1957 a penny was worth arguing about). However, I did feel exonerated and secretly felt that I was the victor in the one-penny case, although because of all the heated arguments I decided it wasn't very safe to announce my victory publicly, and after a few months everyone got back to normal. One thing I still remember about William Dickson's philosophy and wisdom was that he always referred to beans as 'poor man's beef'.

Long before we played any formal team sports, at about four to six years old, we played Cowboys and Indians, or Pirates, with toy guns and wooden swords. The guns became much more dramatic when, now and then, we got caps with real explosive bangs and smoke. But the most effective were our 'tattie guns', which fired small pellets of potato. By sticking the nozzle end of the barrel into a potato, you could load up and fire off your pellets at a target with reasonable accuracy up to ten feet.

Another favourite weapon was the water pistol, which were eventually replaced with washing-up liquid or any other plastic bottle. These had a much greater capacity and firing range. We also made pea-shooters which, when loaded with putty or Plasticine, were much more effective than peas.

An entertaining aspect of being in the upper end of the Burray school was William Dickson's weekly contribution from the *Illustrated London News* magazine. This was serious stuff, but at the age of ten I was reasonably able to understand it. We also had our favourite *The Eagle* comic, with Dan Dare and futuristic space travel and incredible inventions – all in glossy colour. This was only allowed when all our work was done, and done correctly – or done and then corrected, which was the usual option. Time for reading was only allowed in the afternoon. So, if in the afternoon, between two and four, there was no sport, no revision, no library and nothing else, there was either the *London Illustrated* or *The Eagle*, of which there was one of each and about twenty of us. In a really good week, well-organised and with everything just right and timed to perfection, and a lot of luck, you might get a chance to enjoy this reading for its sheer entertainment.

* * *

Another exciting venture, to us at least, was the lighting of grass fires – although to everyone else this was probably regarded as some kind of madness because of the damage and danger it might cause. At the end of summer into early autumn, the grass links became a sort of no-man's land, covered in thick, tufted grass and bulrushes, with a very high, marsh 'bent' grass in some of the low-lying areas. We never burned any heather or trees.

Three or four of us would get together at seven or eight in the evening – when it was getting dark, and on a night that wasn't too windy. We would choose an area of a few acres and use matches. Even if we didn't have a matchbox, any loose matches could be used, since you could use a stone or even the studs on your boots. I don't think safety matches had been invented.

Sometimes to light a fire we experimented with the sun's rays and a magnifying glass or pieces of broken glass, but only when lighting our weekly bonfire rubbish and only during the day, for obvious reasons.

Once a suitable bush had been set alight, upwind from our target area, we used spreaders or tufts of grass as torches to spread a wide front of flames and smoke. Matches were only ever used to start the first fire, or when we had miscalculated the burning conditions or wind direction and had to relocate and start again. Once established on as wide a front as possible, the fire blazed away by itself for four to five hours, destroying everything in its path – although by 'everything' I mean just the grass and a few stray insects. All the birds and animals had taken off long before we got started, what with all our noise and shouting of instructions that went on.

The marsh bent grass was by far the best, giving off huge, hot flames and a roaring crackle that went on for hours, with much less smoke than the other grass. There were two main areas of bent: one down at the reservoir, close to the burn which had been built by the Admiralty and was now disused, except by us; the other was between the sand quarry and the coal-yard. This burning went on for hours until some of the local residents got annoyed by the smoke and flames and chased us. Sometimes we just got tired destroying the environment and went home. The fires somehow burned themselves out before morning.

Nothing would have held us back from returning to the scene of the crime the next day to survey the disaster area with great interest, and to discover what might have been uncovered with all the grass gone, or what creatures had not managed to escape. All we ever found, however, were a few roasted snail shells and a few tin cans and bottles, lying amidst the blackened and devastated wasteland. As I said, any self-respecting animal and bird had flown, with all our noise, and we were careful never to set fires during nesting season, so I suppose we did have our own kind of environmentally-friendly moral code. I also noticed that the next spring, all the grass and bulrushes and wildflowers grew bigger and better, and there was never any shortage of snails or birds and bees and everything else that was always around.

Also in this no-man's land or links area, tinkers used to camp, either as a single family unit or in twos or threes. They would go around the village with packs, selling clothes, toys and domestic items from house to house. We didn't like them very much and I don't think they particularly liked us, so during our fire-lighting missions we tried to avoid them, or at least escape if the fire happened to get out of hand.

Our parents wouldn't have approved of this, although they must have known that we were involved. Certainly, if there were any major inquests, we could always blame it on the other boys who were just as bad as us anyway.

* * *

In the winter during the ice and snow, we sledged and built snowmen. There were two distinct methods of building snowmen. One was to pile up snow with a shovel and then make a head in the same manner – the system used by girls and sissies. We, of course, employed the correct and more strenuous method of taking a small ball of compacted snow and rolling it around until it got bigger and bigger. When it was as high as us, we rolled it into position – that was the body. Then the head was made in a similar way, at about a quarter of the size of the body. This then had to be positioned on top of the body. Usually this involved three or four of us standing round the snowman, each thinking his method of positioning the head was best, and nothing quite working right. The head often ended up back on the ground in a thousand pieces. Usually after the third attempt, the masterpiece was declared a resounding success.

Next, the snowman was given a face and arms. A carrot made a good nose, with lumps of coal for eyes and small coals for teeth. It sometimes got a scarf, though very seldom a hat, with two branches for arms and sometimes different coloured stones for buttons down the front of the body. Our snowman could sometimes last up to two months, despite wind, rain and sun, until it was just a small icy heap on the ground.

One year we got so much snow it went up to the eaves on the roof, and even the snowplough couldn't get through all the roads. We got two or three days off school that year. Council workers dug out big blocks of snow and ice to clear as much as possible, moving the blocks along the edges of the roads. It was fun to walk along the roads, up to the height of the roofs without sinking in too much. We even took some of those blocks and built an igloo, which looked just like the real thing. It was big enough for three or four of us to get into at the same time.

With the snow that year, the ponds froze over with thick ice, great for skating and sliding on, although we never owned actual ice-skates. And with snow around, snowball fights were the order of the day, sometimes on an individual basis with every boy for himself, but sometimes it erupted into all-out war between two teams.

Another adventure for the snow involved the wild rabbits. Although eating rabbits was a commonplace occurrence, it was the excitement of catching them that was the main attraction to us. Rabbit-hunting in winter meant tracking them in the snow, and it was always done during daylight. Having followed the rabbit's footprints until they came to a dead end at a clump of grass or a heather bush, we used our weapons to maximum effect – that is, a wooden club similar to a baseball bat – and surprised the rabbit by beating down on the bush to catch it unawares. This highly sophisticated method did in fact yield one or two rabbits in about six hours of hunting. However, four out of every five managed to run off before we could catch them, and once these rabbits were aware of us, it was almost impossible for us to track them again.

When I was about twelve or thirteen, an outbreak of myxomatosis developed among the rabbit population. It made the rabbits blind and crippled, and they eventually died an agonising death after about a month. After this we never hunted or ate rabbits again. Although officially this was hailed as a natural disease that rabbit populations get from time to time, we were convinced it had been introduced and spread by someone, or some group, to decimate the Orkney rabbit population. Though there were lots of recriminations, I never felt that we ever got the truth. However, I'm glad to say there are still wild rabbits in Orkney today.

* * *

As I remember it, the main event days in Orkney included Christmas Day, Boxing Day, Hogmanay and New Year, April Fool's, Good Friday, Easter Monday, Halloween, Guy Fawkes and Armistice or Poppy Day.

Christmas Day was the biggest highlight of our year; sometimes we even had a white Christmas. We had special events at school leading up to it, including the traditional exchange of Christmas cards at school – between twenty and thirty cards each year, if I remember rightly.

Another occasion was the year-end games at school, a grand knock-out event with board or card games supplied by the teachers. In fact it usually started way back in October. The idea was for all of us to participate at different levels and the games included Snap, Old Maid, Ludo, Snakes & Ladders, Monopoly, Sorry, Scrabble, Risk, Dominos and Checkers. Each game went on for approximately two months, in the afternoons. On competition days, under strict rules and conditions, and at the final knock-out after eliminating everyone else, the two survivors had to compete against each other with an absolute final game. The winner then got the game to keep. Over the years, I did win a few games – it was a great feeling of achievement.

Into the second week of December, we started putting up decorations at home and at school. We sometimes managed to get a real Christmas tree, and also real holly and mistletoe.

When we were young we always wrote our lists to Santa Claus at the North Pole. The list was then burned in the fire and the paper ash, on which you could still decipher the writing, was sucked up the lum with the draught. Of course, we all knew that this went straight to Santa at the North Pole. Then, early on Christmas morning, there was great excitement to see what Santa had brought each of us.

As we went to the Kirk every Sunday, we never looked on Christmas Day as a major churchgoing day. Once home from the service, we enjoyed a huge Christmas dinner at about one o'clock. This was always roast turkey or roast goose with some other meat, usually roast beef, followed by plum pudding – with sixpences in it – and custard. The whole Christmassy excitement of playing games and making up jigsaw puzzles carried on until the next day, Boxing Day, a day that, for us, really meant clearing up and getting back to normal.

The first day of January was always significant to our family; it was also Gavin's birthday. However, New Year's Eve – Hogmanay – was always an important event in Orkney, with everyone – the men that is – doing their first-footing. This was a cleverly disguised excuse to go round with a piece of coal and a bottle or half-bottle of whisky, wishing people luck and visiting as many folk as possible, perhaps having a drink or two, just before – and as long as possible after – the clock struck midnight. Then, of course, there was the traditional entertainment, with everyone singing – or trying to sing – 'Auld Lang Syne'.

Whether you had recovered or not, we always had New Year's dinner at one o'clock, with everyone sitting around the table. It was usually roast goose or chicken, and another roast meat, with gravy, roast potatoes, peas, carrots and all the trimmings, plus trifle for dessert.

In Orkney the major event of the year takes place in Kirkwall on New Year's Day. It's the Ba' game, which isn't really a game at all – more like small-scale civil war. There are four games played every year: the boys' and men's games on Christmas Day, and the boys' (up to age sixteen) and men's games on New Year's Day. The final game was the most important one.

There are always two teams – the 'Uppies' and the 'Doonies' – and the game is won when one side scores. For the Uppies to triumph, they have to score by hitting the ba' against a wall past the top end of Broad Street (the main street in Kirkwall), up past St Magnus Cathedral. For the Doonies to gain the upper hand, they have to get the ba' into the harbour bay. At the stroke of one o'clock on St Magnus Cathedral, the ba' – which weighs about three pounds and is a cork-filled leather ball about the size of a football – is thrown into the throng. There are no other rules. The ba' can be kicked, thrown, passed forward or back, run with over roofs and along walls – anything goes. Each team can be anything from two to six hundred players, aged from eighteen to eighty. The spectators, who might also become players – and vice-versa – number in their thousands all along the route. The game lasted anything from three to nine hours, but it had to finish with one mob scoring. The actual goal-scorer became the hero of the day and the ba' was his to keep for ever. Every new game had a new ba', specially made by the official ba'-making guild of Orkney.

Once a Doonie or an Uppie, that was it for life, even for generations. There were never turncoats or traitors, or if there were they were never heard of again.

During this madness and mayhem, all normal thinking was suspended. Shopowners took maximum defensive measures and boarded up and barricaded everything they could. The main street in Kirkwall is cobbled and although ironically named Broad Street, for such a narrow street. It has one tall, protected, tree half-way along, in the centre of town. Most of the other streets are modern tarred roads, and the harbour is right at the edge of the town. All the original buildings and houses are stone built, with slate roofs, and the roads are very good, and wide enough for cars and buses to drive through. However, on the day of the game it was considered not particularly clever to park your vehicle too near to the action.

April Fool's Day was a great day for us bairns and we would go around telling absolutely outrageous stories to each other, or get someone to look for – or do – something really silly, and then shout 'goki-goki!' or 'April fool'! This, of course, worked best on anyone who hadn't remembered what day it was.

Our birthdays were also considered special days and, as it so happened, the three of us were quite close together – me in October, Ian in December, Gavin in January, with Christmas in between. Our mother would bake a special cake with icing and candles – one for every year, stuck in special holders. The candles would be lit, and you made a secret wish and had to blow all the candles out with one breath, which we always seemed to manage. We usually got a few presents, and four or five birthday cards.

Easter was also a special time, mainly because of the school holidays. We also got chocolate Easter eggs and hot cross buns, and hard-boiled hens' eggs which, when we were very young, we painted and rolled down the grass slopes in the links. Because there is a Sunday between Good Friday and Easter Monday, this was one of the special times when we went from Sunday School to the big Kirk service – which of course was all in the same building. After the Easter service we all went home to tuck into a special dinner, a bit like Christmas again (I don't think we had to walk round the square at Easter and Christmas).

As Halloween was on 31 October, and only five days before Guy Fawkes, we kind of combined the two occasions when collecting for the 'Guy'. We went from door-to-door asking or begging for a penny for the guy, and of course hoping for more. The 'more' never seemed to happen very often, but we sometimes got a glass of ginger wine and a bit of home-made shortbread, which was reasonable, I suppose.

On Halloween there was the dooking, when apples were floating about in a tub of water and you had to catch one with your teeth – no hands allowed. Or an apple would be strung from the ceiling on a piece of string and – the same – you had to catch it with your teeth – again no hands allowed.

We also made neepie lanterns and this was for our night-time ventures. These were made with the biggest neeps we could find from raiding the farmer's fields. Sometimes the big yellow ones were almost the size of a football.

Having made off with our prize neep, we now had to turn it into a scary Halloween lantern. It took hours. First, after cleaning the earth off, we removed the root and shaw leaves. We then sliced the top off – which became the lid. The biggest job was to hollow out the neep with knives, spoons and any other gadgets you thought might help. The neep was actually quite good to eat raw, but I think the rest ended up in the hen food and was also fed to the rabbits. When our neep was completely hollow, we would cut a fierce looking face in the one side – with teeth, eyes and nose. We then fixed a candle in the base, put the lid back on, made two holes for a string handle, and our neepie lantern was ready for action.

Although we burned these lanterns all night, we never ran out of candles because we made our own – dozens at a time – from the mixtures of candlewax and beeswax that were always being washed up on the beach. We had all sorts of different moulds and string for wicks, depending on the type of candle we wanted.

Halloween also involved the daring 'big boy' stuff when we went out to annoy people at night. Looking back, however, it didn't really seem all that daring or annoying, to be honest. When you are eight or nine though, this was the big time. It all took place between seven and nine, when it was pitch dark. We would do things like ring the doorbell at the front door of a house, while another boy would knock at the back door – then we would run and hide across the road and watch. The folk would come out at both doors, look around and go back inside. If we got a really good response – someone looking puzzled or annoyed – we would tie some cans or bottles to the door knob and do it again. Then if the response was even greater, with threats and trying to catch us, we would escape to the next house across the road.

This 'big boy' stuff could also involve taking off gates and putting them on other people's roofs, or moving wheelbarrows or flower pots from one house to another. Although we made sure we were never around the morning after to see what mayhem had ensued, we did have a look within a day or two. By that time all the owners had eventually sorted themselves out and everything seemed to go back to normal.

Guy Fawkes too was such a major highlight. Although the

evening of 5 November was the time for lighting the bonfire and setting off the fireworks, the activities started well back in August. This gave us three months to collect all sorts of combustible material for the biggest and best bonfire of the year – to beat all previous years. First prize was as many rubber tyres as possible – the bigger the better – usually car tyres. If we could get a truck or even a tractor tyre, this was even better. The two main places for tyre collection was at the two garages – Douglas's and Tait's. Since Ruthie Douglas was our friend, this helped to influence the decision sometimes, but Alfie Tait and his brother usually got involved in their own activities, so this source didn't work out very well. Sometimes we found tyres at the beach, and in a really good Guy Fawkes collection, we could have as many as ten tyres.

At the beach we collected 'roasted pigs' – huge, dried-out divots washed from the cliffs and banks, about the size of pillows. We also got wood, boxes and other stuff from the beach. We went round all the shops and houses and got cardboard boxes, packing material, clothes, shoes, tree branches, straw bales and even bed mattresses. All of this was loaded onto our trolleys and taken home. The durable materials – like tyres, branches, roasted pigs and straw bales – could be piled immediately outside at the fire site. All the dry stuff – paper and cardboard – had to be packed and stacked into one of our sheds until the actual day of Guy Fawkes, because it rained just about every day during October and November. The clothes were used to make the 'Guy' – stuffed with paper and straw – as real-looking as possible – even with a face and a hat.

Although we always had our own Guy Fawkes bonfire with several of our friends, the competition also collected for their own fires. So there were several going at the same time on Burray.

On the evening of 5th November – and it was strangely almost always a fair night weather-wise, usually without any rain – we would get home from school and immediately start packing and piling up our Guy Fawkes fire. About seven o' clock, we used matches to light this huge heap at five or six different places at the base, with the Guy sitting at the top on a tyre, about twelve feet above the ground. Within fifteen minutes we had a roaring fire blazing away – very hot and bright – which carried on burning until midnight.

Now, with the fire going, we set off our fireworks. The sky rockets were always placed in a bottle and pointed as vertical as possible and then lit – whooshing into the sky with bursts of colourful sparks as they went on their way. The bangers and hand-held sparklers we set off at random, and some Roman Candles we could also hold, but Volcanoes that light up the night – and other flares – were stuck into the ground at a fair distance. Jumping Jacks always seemed to follow you around, no matter how far you threw them, and the Catherine Wheels always got nailed to a door or fence pole. We could also see the competition's fires and rockets

All events came to an end at about ten. We then had tea, lemonade, cakes, even ginger or strawberry wine.

Despite the late night and all the excitement, we still got up very early the next morning to check the fire before school – if it was a school day. Better if it was a Saturday or Sunday – then we had time to look at the still-smouldering heap of ash, with the steel wire from the tyres and springs from the mattresses, and other interesting stuff. Then we would also have time to try and find the burned-out rockets and see how far they had gone, and to check for any fireworks that still had some life in them.

In the week after Guy Fawkes, on 11 November, there was what we knew as 'Poppy Day' – never referred to as Remembrance or Armistice Day, or anything else. The school and community took this day very seriously indeed. We, the big boys at the Burray school, were allocated poppy distribution areas, with a specific quantity of red silk poppies and a collection tin. This task had to be carried out the Saturday before the 11th, and if 11 November fell on a Saturday, then it would be done on the Saturday prior. In the Orkney Isles it would probably be raining and windy by this time of the year, or at best cold and windy. Nonetheless, the task was undertaken with great determination.

So, with duffel coat fastened with bone buttons that looked like wart-hog teeth, hood over your head, pack of poppies, cash tin hanging from the handlebars, bike in gear (it only had one gear), I was off – freezing cold and wet (no gloves, I never wore gloves until I got much older). When you're nine or ten, this was really hard-going. I always went alone and assumed that everyone else did likewise. To get around fifty or so houses, spread miles apart, on your bike, some on dirt roads, took from about nine in the morning till thee in the afternoon, and that was the whole Saturday gone. On looking back, at least I can feel that my small contribution was for a good cause.

* * *

As kids going to Sunday School, we usually had the standard fire-and-brimstone type of teachers. However, Sandy Wylie was different, in as much as we were even allowed to voice our own opinions and ideas on matters of religion and the greater power. One Sunday, during these discussion sessions, the topic was 'Why is religion important?' We were generally taught that the reason was to guide us through life correctly, in order to reach our ultimate destination in a just and peaceful manner. And to achieve this, we had to have a belief in the greater power that existed. To emphasise this, Sandy gave each of us a piece of chalk and asked us to draw a straight line on the blackboard. Then with all twelve or thirteen lines on the board, Sandy took his a long ruler and drew a straight line. We were then invited to decide which line was the straightest. Compared to our squiggles there was no contest, and the unanimous decision was that his was the only true straight line. Sandy Wylie thus confirmed to us that, in life, it was not possible to go in a straight line without a ruler as your guide.

Although most of our official education came from school, my mother was also a source of information. I remember one night, sitting together while she was doing a repair job on someone's pyjamas by feeding elastic through the waist-band with a strange blunt needle. When I asked her what the needle was, she said it was a bodkin, I thought this was a hilariously funny word, and since I was never very good at spelling I asked her to spell it. Another funny word that came up in conversation was 'firkin', which I also thought was very funny. However, as I advanced a bit at school and began to learn more, all our sums and mathematics were in imperial measures and units – so I learnt that a firkin was the official name for a quarter-barrel which was equivalent to nine gallons, and a barrel was therefore equal to thirty-six. Anyway, looking back, my mother's teaching actually had more of an effect on me from a 'learning and remembering' point of view than all the official methods. Teaching by rote was mostly just pure drudgery.

My mother also said that girls were usually better at spelling than boys. Perhaps that explained my worst subject at school – dictation. Every Wednesday Mrs Lilian Gray would read out a story and we had to write it down with all the correct spelling and punctuation.

To help figure this all out, we learned mental arithmetic at school, up to the twelve times table. This made it easy for mental calculation up to the twenty-two times table – that is, by multiplying the figure by twelve and adding that to the figure multiplied by ten, you had your twenty-two times table answer. Since all this teaching took place during the era BC (that is, before calculators), we had to make do with ready-reckoner tables and slide-rules to help us with our calculations.

*   *   *

One of our great achievements as boys was the building of major sea-going rafts. Design and size was totally dependent on availability of materials, and all materials had to be collected and transported to the construction site – which was also the launch site – at the top of the beach, well above the high-tide mark. The main components of the raft were steel oil drums, preferably the forty-five gallon variety. The ideal design required eight drums, each approximately three feet high with a diameter of one foot. This, to our mind, intelligent design would be constructed with the drums lying flat on their side, using four sets of drums, each consisting of two drums laid end-to-end.

After collecting the eight oil drums, boards of wood, pitch, nails, tools and all necessary equipment, we commenced the construction, assembling the flat top of the raft first. There were no formal measurements made, but everything was generally sized-up to fit, based on the planks and boards available to accommodate the drums underneath. The raft was, in effect, built upside down. Having got the basic top deck together with thousands of nails, the drums were then positioned and held in place with an elaborate criss-cross wooden structure.

However, there were two rather important aspects that were almost overlooked and one was the condition of the oil drums. Ideally they should be water-tight, each having two screw caps securely fitted. The standard of our drums was less than ideal. Only three of the eight were watertight, while the rest were rusty and holed with caps missing. This was considered only a slight setback as we got to work with a pot of pitch, heated over a huge wood fire on the beach. Soon any flaws, fractures and deterio-rated parts were fixed up as good as new and all caps sealed.

The other oversight was the weight of the completed raft, which was far heavier than anticipated. However, after much heated discussion, it was decided that the extra weight would be advantageous for stability, which, as things turned out, may have been right. After about a week of work, and with oars, ropes, an anchor and everything organised, we were ready to launch.

Being in the middle of our school holidays in July, the weather had been really good up until that point. However, on launch day it became windy and dull, but there was no rain. As usual we couldn't wait and had to launch, with much difficulty, against the onshore waves. Surprisingly the raft held together and we – the three of us – clambered aboard and managed to get about a hundred yards offshore, despite being battered by the incoming waves for about half an hour. We ended up washed ashore just under half a mile along the beach, completely exhausted. Sailing was abandoned for the day and the half-ton raft was hauled up to the top of the beach in readiness for a better day.

The following Friday was declared a good day and by two in the afternoon, with no wind, the sea was calm like a mirror. The tide was going out – perfect. We got the oars, ropes, fishing tackle and cockle-bait and launched. By four, at low tide and in ideal conditions, we sailed out and got alongside the Barrier.

Everything seemed to be going well and we could see right to the bottom through the crystal clear water – about twenty fathoms. With two of us fishing and one manoeuvring the raft, things were going according to plan. Then we started listing to one side – one or two of the drums were taking in water. So, given our vast experience of sailing, and buoyed up with the notion that we knew how to handle things that could go wrong, we decided to continue the fishing while making for harbour. We did actually make it ashore without any further mishap, but to be honest it wasn't particularly safe. The raft was permanently grounded, and eventually dismantled and stockpiled to be used in future inventions.

From that day, we borrowed a rowing boat, a small flat-bottomed dinghy known as a flatty. It could reasonably take a crew of four – one rowing, one navigating (or arguing) and two fishing (or throwing stones at anything that moved or wouldn't move). From this flatty we could swim by anchoring and getting in and out without tipping over, and sometimes we would just hang on the back and get pulled along by whoever was lucky enough to be rowing at the time.

When on dry land, we often made weapons for sport. This usually resulted in either a catapult or bow and arrow. The catapults came in various forms, usually cut out of a flat board of wood, since the conventional Y-shaped part of a tree branch was not readily available because there are very few trees in Orkney. The alternative was to make the 'Y' part out of metal, but even this had many variations. The sling was always rubber from a car or bicycle tube. The catapults actually worked well and we became great shots at hitting cans and bottles, using small stones as ammunition.

The bow and arrow came in two basic types. One was made with a thin bamboo rod about three feet long, using string or nylon fishing line. The other – made from a high tension steel rod, two and a half feet long and curved – was the best method. Arrows were either wood or bamboo about fifteen inches long, and tipped with lead at the business end. This was our own ingenious addition, made with commonly used lead-covered 'twin' electric cable. By pulling out the cable, we effectively had a lead tube, which we cut into one-inch lengths and fitted to the pointed end of our arrows and hammered it flat. To hold it onto the arrow at the bow-string end, we cut a 'V' to fit the string. We tried some feathers and other flights on them, but this didn't make any improvement.

Other hobbies included making wooden model boats with sails, and launching them from one island to the next – which worked fine. The only problem was finding your boat before someone else did, since it could take overnight, depending on weather and sea conditions.

'Snoring Bones' was another favourite game. These were made in all shapes and sizes, but always constructed from a piece of flat wood, metal or plastic, and cut in a round disk about the diameter of an orange. This flat disk could have smooth or serrated edges and random holes of various sizes, but it had to have two holes in the centre like a button. String was then put through the two button holes and the ends tied together to form a loop at each side of your snoring bone. Each one was about twelve inches, from the snoring bone to the hand-held loop. The snoring bone was now wound up by turning it over and over on itself until the loops of string on both sides were well twisted up. To activate your snoring bone you pulled your hands apart while holding the two loops, and you could continue with your device snoring away all day, if you had the time or inclination to keep it going.

One day Ruthie came round to our house, walking on stilts.

Since we had never even seen stilts before, this looked very unnatural. It seemed strange that she didn't just fall off, because as far as we could see it wasn't possible to stand on two sticks with base feet no bigger than matchboxes. After much discussion, we eventually fathomed out the intricate physics of stilts and after a few days, had manufactured our own set. They worked so well that the novelty lasted for months.

Another strange device that appeared to defy gravity was the Hula Hoop, which was a national craze about this time. We became quite expert at defying gravity.

Air guns or 'slug guns' – we never referred to them as air guns – were another favourite. The first slug gun I ever saw was Ian's. He got one at Kirkwall when he was about twelve. This was a Diana pistol of 0.177 calibre, and it could shoot lead slugs or pellets and steel darts for target-shooting. We became expert shots with the steel darts, aiming at paper bull's-eye targets. When I was eleven, I got an air rifle, also 0.177 calibre. Although I used this rifle for target-shooting at tin cans and bottles, with this particular gun I could now do some big-time hunting.

In the first year my trophies ranged from one mouse (I think I waited up all night until it came out to get my strategically placed cheese), and one sparrow (that got caught eating the hens' food), and one starling that was unfortunate enough to be sitting on the telegraph wires within sight. About a year or so later I upgraded to a 0.22 slug gun B.S.A. air rifle. To be honest, I didn't really cause too much death and destruction with my new rifle; although I was obliged to hunt small rodents for my crow until it learned the ways of the wilds.

Bicycles were also central to my childhood. With the long, dark winter nights on Orkney, light was a big issue and we had lights on our bikes (well, sometimes). These were either powered by battery or a dynamo, the ultimate in free electric power. The three of us rigged up a dynamo on to a sort of revolving weather vane, and Dad made a wooden propeller to drive the dynamo with wind-power. Because Orkney has enough wind to run the entire planet, we had continual free electricity to power our six-volt light-bulb, and so our shed had perpetual light. This invention proved to be a great success – we were years ahead of the rest of the world with our wind-powered electricity.

Another successful project included the making of an electric blanket. During the 1950s in Orkney it was common practice to use a rubber hot-water bottle, so the advent of an electric blanket was a major leap for heating the bed. To us, the invention of the electric blanket wasn't important; we had already made one ourselves. Dad had somehow got his hands on the element wires, controls and plugs and all the necessary components. All we had to do was get two double-bed sized blankets, lay the elements onto one blanket, get the ends, controls and plugs all connected up, sew the element in position in a looping grill type format, then sew the other blanket on top. Hey presto! – a genuine-looking electric blanket which actually worked, without anyone being electrocuted or anything set on fire. Although this was a roaring success, we never made another one. Who knows, this original blanket may still be working somewhere to this day.

* * *

I was given my first bicycle at about the age of eight and that feeling of independence, of balancing on my bike unaided, was the most memorable and exhilarating experience ever. It was also the start of my career in business.

Even before I got the bike, I had learned that collecting non-ferrous scrap metal, such as copper, brass, lead and aluminium, was a way to make money. So in my own small way, with my brothers – although really in competition with my brothers – I ventured into the scrap-metal business, and I became, in my own opinion, the ultimate expert. In the 1950s no one ever talked about the importance of environment, and the sea was regarded as a natural waste-disposable system. If you consider that barely ten years earlier, it seemed to be ongoing practice to sink ships and wreck everything in the name of war, well throwing a tin can or glass bottle into the sea was regarded as normal and indeed insignificant. Thus it was that I could walk along the beach back then and it was like a scrap-metal yard waiting to be picked over.

We collected copper wire and sometimes cable wire which could be stripped of its rubber or PCV insulation, or just simply burned. There were also old brass handles and window catches, tops of lamps and old primus stoves, lead sinkers and bits of roof sheets and aluminium, floats, pots, kettles, even light-bulbs (that we would break to get at the brass base). When we found good aluminium buoys about the size of a football, we used to send them off to a dealer, whose name and address we found in the *Exchange & Mart* newpaper. This Aberdeen-based company paid all postage costs, and we received instant payment by money-order of half a crown each. We didn't find many buoys, but it was good when we did.

The collection of non-ferrous scrap-metal continued in all sorts of ingenious ways and warranted the purchase of our own weighing scale. This was a major breakthrough, because up till then we had to trust the dealer and take his word for the weight of our hard earned spoils, and since we got paid by the pound weight, every pound counted. Although we thought we were blessed with great bargaining skills, holding out to the end for the maximum best price, there really wasn't much to negotiate with. There was only one main dealer and the price was set. Our dealer did however suggest that we might get into the ferrous iron and steel scrap-metal business, to supplement our thriving non-ferrous business. We took his advice.

During our ventures along the beach, we would throw tins and bottles into the sea and throw stones at them. Breaking a glass bottle in the sea was great fun, although not very sensible – as I was to discover to my detriment some time later.

Talking of glass bottles, we also branched out into the soft-drink business, collecting various lemonade bottles for the deposit. This was quite good business at sixpence for a big bottle and threepence for a small one. Because I could do unlimited travel on my bike, and since formal waste disposal and environ-mental control was twenty years away (in Burray anyway), people acted in a manner which nowadays would be regarded as irresponsible. Empty bottles were often thrown out of car windows onto grass verges at the side of the road, or could be found discarded on the beach, and just about anywhere. As it appeared that it was too much bother for folk to return empty bottles to the shops, this was easy pickings for me. However, I rather felt that my enterprise was not a monopoly. There was definitely competition around and it wasn't going to turn me into a millionaire.

Looking around for other opportunities, I ventured into gardening. Although hard work, it proved to be quite a good business. It only involved cutting grass and mowing lawns. I already deployed my services free of charge at home – using a manual lawnmower and a scythe for the long grass – and I received a request for my horticultural services from our new neighbours next door. As luck would have it, they had a brand new electric Flymo lawn-mower. Of course I had never even heard of a Flymo, let alone seen one, but since it was assumed that I was knew what I was doing, I immediately negotiated and concluded a contract. This involved doing the lawn weekly, front and back garden, at half a crown per area; it would take about two hours to complete for the five-shilling deal. When I got the Flymo plugged in and switched on, the job was more pleasure than hard work. Of course I never admitted that to anyone, but the Flymo floated along and cut the grass so effortlessly that all I had to do was hold the handlebars, switch the controls and walk around behind it. Indeed this gardening business was so good that I had schemes and plans to expand and branch out, but the idea never really blossomed.

* * *

One of the things that made Orkney, if not famous, but at least a group of islands that were known and recognisable on the map, was its sea-faring history. Some of this concerned the two World Wars.

During World War I the entire German naval fleet of seventy-four ships was sunk (scuttled) in Scapa Flow in June 1919, without any loss of life, indeed without the Royal Navy suffering even a scratch on its own paintwork. If this is how the story ended, it would have been the greatest sea victory of all time before and since, but that is not the whole story.

In November 1918 the German fleet was interned in the Scapa Flow sound. According to some legislation in the League of Nations rule book of what is allowed and what is not allowed during a war (killing people it appears is always allowed, but some more serious offences are not allowed), taking the enemy fleet prisoner was permissable, with the proviso that the entire crew was allowed to remain on board their ships at anchor and be supplied with all humanitarian needs of food, water, medical supplies and whatever else necessary. Anyway, this holiday at sea lasted from November 1918 until June 1919 while the League of Nations and British Admirality did a lot of political posturing and held endless committee meetings – sick of their extended stay, the enemy decided to disembark so that they could spend the rest of their lives on dry land.

Oddly enough this wasn't permitted, because it was the job of the enemy crews to look after their ships until it could be decided at some future committee meeting what to do with seventy-four warships. These, by the way, in terms of warships, were the most modern the world had ever seen – none of them was more than five years old.

However, before the Allied boffins could get together for yet another meeting to decide the fate of the fleet, the Germans took matters into their own hands, having gathered that all hope of escape was futile. During one perfect summer evening, on 21 June 1919, the German crews simultaneously opened the stopcocks on their ships, as mutually arranged, flooding and thereby sinking their entire fleet, under the very nose of the Royal Navy.

And having scuttled their ships, it was now the job of the Royal Navy to rescue all the German crews and take them safely ashore.

Until this saga of June 1919, the biggest Royal Navy disaster concerning Scapa Flow was on 9 July 1917, when the battleship H.M.S *Vanguard* was sunk with a loss of over eight hundred crew members. Again this was achieved without any enemy involvement, by someone or something interfering with explosives in the magazine which blew up the whole ship – it sank within minutes.

Although such tragedies accounted for such terrible loss of life and resources, the events themselves probably raised a general awareness of where and what the Orkney Islands were. However, it was approximately twenty-five years later that greater impressions were made on the international scene.

The British Admiralty now decided to use Scapa Flow as one of its main bases for the Royal Naval fleet. Scapa Flow, in fact, is a very large expanse of sea and the sound is surrounded, indeed practically enclosed by, a circular chain of islands. It is thus a natural anchorage and is well-placed strategically – and geographically – in the Atlantic Ocean. On the one side (west) is the Atlantic Ocean, and to the east is the North Sea and Europe, with the Arctic Circle to the north, and mainland Britain to the south. There is no access to Scapa Flow from the north, however, this being totally blocked by the main island of Pomona. At the time, the available access was only one of three ways: from the west between Pomona and Hoy island (the second biggest island), from the south end of Hoy island and South Ronaldsay, and from the east on both sides of Burray – i.e. between Burray and Pomona, and Burray and South Ronaldsay. This creates the complete circle.

To reinforce the security of the Scapa Flow base, the Navy used steel anti-submarine nets and sea mines (huge explosive devices designed to sink any sea-going craft that came into contact with them). A sea mine looks like an oversized floating football, about four foot in diameter, with antenna all over it, which was anchored to the sea bed with chains and fixed to float at any pre-determined level in the sea between the bottom and the surface. Theoretically they would be difficult to avoid.

However, during the confusion of World War II, not everything worked according to theory. A German U-boat managed to get into Scapa Flow, and torpedoed and sank the battleship H.M.S. *Royal Oak*. The ship sank almost immediately with the loss of hundreds of men, while the U-boat escaped from the Royal Navy stronghold without detection.

This transgression was taken seriously by the British Admiralty, who immediately commandeered and expropriated about twenty-five sea-going vessels in the area with little warning to the owners or crew, in the name of the war effort. The crews hurriedly disembarked with any belongings they could carry. The commandeered ships, all in decent sea-going condition, were immediately positioned strategically between the islands – at the access routes, and then sunk with strategically-placed explosives.

It was thought that the sinking of ships in the main access channels between the islands (though leaving one or two main routes open which would be heavily guarded) would ensure that Scapa Flow remained a safe haven. But the plan was flawed. In the event, some ships were blown completely in two with the bow and stern sections sinking several hundred feet apart. Others didn't sink quick enough and ended up in the wrong place; some even ran aground.

Nonetheless, the final result was an improvement to the defences of Scapa Flow but this was deemed not good enough by the First Sea Lord of the Admiralty, who happened to be Sir Winston Churchill. He demanded that the east approach to Scapa Flow be permanently sealed off by linking all five islands with solid concrete barriers – to make shipping movement permanently impossible. A feasibility study was done by the engineering contractors Balfour Beatty – the company my father worked for. However, with Britain now at the height of the World War II, there was now a shortage of everything, including labour. So Churchill advocated that Italian prisoners-of-war detained in Orkney should be used to provide labour.

To improve the ambulance services, certain strategic (that is, dangerous area) roads had to be built and/or improved. The most important ones were those around Britain's major Naval bases – in particular at Scapa Flow – so this was given priority. Since most of the road links around the base there did not exist at the time, they would have to be built from scratch. To build a road from one island to another, there are three possibilities: under the water, over the water or through the water. The under options – a tunnel or a bridge – were never really considered. Given previous feasibility studies by Balfour Beatty, the option to go through the water – with a causeway link from island to island, and with a road capable of taking two-way ambulance traffic – was chosen.

Since it was acceptable to utilise P.O.W.s in humanitarian efforts, Winston Churchill got his way to use the Italians to build the now famous Churchill Barriers which might have been built without roads on top.

Balfour Beatty got to work using their own personnel – which included my father – the necessary equipment and logistics, and the Italian prisoners, and all under control of the British Admiralty and, of course, Winston Churchill.

The four Barriers were completed over several years, using locally-quarried rocks and stone, and locally-manufactured concrete blocks of five-ton and ten-ton weights. Thus the link road causeways were created, each approximately three-quarters of a mile long, through the sea in depths of up to eighteen fathoms in very rough seas and strong currents. The network finally linked the main island of Pomona to Lamb Holm (Barrier No. 1), Lamb Holm to Glimps Holm (Barrier No. 2), Glimps Holm to Burray (Barrier No. 3), and Burray to South Ronaldsay (Barrier No. 4). The major lifting and transport equipment used in all this barrier construction included Blondin cableway cranes, derricks, mobile cranes (Rustin & Bucyrus) and crawler cranes (Bucyrus Erie), and multi-steel wheeled and tyred Scammell trucks and trailers, plus dumpers and other trucks.

While building the Churchill Barriers, the Italian prisoners were housed at camp 60 on the island of Lamb Holm. During their stay, they also created the now famous Italian chapel, with a statue of St George and the Dragon at the entrance. The building of this magnificent chapel took place due to the inspiration and leadership of Domenico Chiocchetti, a prisoner with great vision and artistic capability. On being given two Nissen huts by the War Office inspector of prisoner-of-war camps, with the idea that the men could use one as a school and the other as a church, the two huts were instead joined end to end to make a chapel, with the blessing of the British camp commandant and padre. At the end of the War, the Italian chapel was left in the capable hands of Mr Sutherland-Graeme, Lord Lieutenant of Orkney.

Although the Churchill Barriers were a resounding success and prevented enemy sea-craft from entering Scapa Flow again, the block-ships were left where they had been sunk and in some cases were very close to the Churchill Barriers. This measure was beneficial to us as kids, however.

My first involvement with the block ships was probably ten or so years after they were sunk. When I was about four or five, I had my first experience of the ships when my father took me to see the *Carron*, which was really the only ship we could get to – and then only at very low tide. This great ship appeared absolutely complete to me. Parallel alongside the Barrier, completely upright with the bow facing the beach and the stern out in the deep water. You could still see the anchor, the anchor chains, winches, masts and funnel and even the engine room, which was always flooded even at low tide. I could climb up the steel ladders to the top deck and onto the bridge, and with my bamboo rod and fixed-line and hook (using limpets as bait), I could fish in the flooded holds, a bit like fishing in a giant-sized goldfish bowl with two-foot sides all round it. It was completely safe and I couldn't fall in if I tried. This is where I got my first taste of dulse seaweed – which my father said was good for me. Maybe it was, but it was also my last taste, and I didn't go out of my way to try it again.

The holds were swarming with fish – and anything from four

to ten inches long was a monstrous sea-creature to me at that time. I would often catch as many as a dozen and take them home to eat, much to the delight of the cats who were always waiting eagerly in anticipation. Even ten years after the *Carron* was sunk, all the spoils were pretty much gone before I got a chance to check it out. Nonetheless, in my scrabbles around the cabins – which still had doors which you could open and close – I found several coins, such as a few pennies and half-pennies, a threepenny bit and, my best, a sixpence covered in rust from lying on the steel cabin deck.

However, a few years later for me, while still fishing off the *Carron*, I spotted the potential of scrap metal. Even fifteen or so years after sinking, there were still lead-covered cables, brass brackets and brass hinges to be had. There was also a huge bronze propeller, permanently under water, and way out of my league. These ships were a free-for-all, with apparently no owner, or at least no one obviously in charge or remotely interested. Although officially, they were still deemed to be Admiralty property. So I was completely at the tail end, trying to pick up what was either too difficult, or just not even worth the bother to anyone else. And after I got to work with my hammer and chisel, and all the wrecking tools that I could muster, some lead-covered cable, brass brackets, and even half a porthole cover were salvaged from the deep.

Now around the time I was ten, the *Carron* was attacked by some professional wreckers and scrap-dealers. This went on for a year or so, during which time they managed, with their frog-men and explosives, to get one propeller off. They also broke down a mast, cut up cabins and decks, capstans, and parts of the engine room with oxy-acetylene gas torches. (Who knows, perhaps I was the one to start their industry and ideas by selling them the scrap in the beginning.)

The dealers' scrap was transported to the top of the beach on a cableway-and-pulley system they had rigged up with a diesel-winch which was really an improvised and modified Massey Ferguson tractor. They then loaded up all the steel scrap onto trucks and piled it up on the Burray Pier. After about a year, their hectic activity ended as abruptly as it had begun, leaving their cableway system behind them.

So we still had our *Carron*, not too badly damaged – and we now had our own ship-to-shore system. Although unstable and highly dangerous, we didn't let such minor details deter us and we carried on using this cableway-and-pulley winch for years without any major mishaps – other than getting stranded half-way between ship and shore one day, dangling on the end of a rope thirty feet in the air.

What also survived for many years was the heap of scrap iron and steel on our pier which was either abandoned or impounded, but eventually disappeared.

* * *

By the time I was eleven, our baby sister Fiona was three years of age, Colin was seven, Gavin thirteen and Ian fifteen. Ian had joined the Boys' Brigade and had become more enterprising, and, although still at school, was working part-time on View Forth Farm. This job seemed to involve every Saturday and I think some Sundays and some week nights as well, and gave Ian a chance to drive the Dexter tractor.

Now the agricultural seasons are a major part of farming on Orkney. During the spring, there is always ploughing, harrowing and fertilising, and crop planting. The crops are grain, mainly oats and barley, and grass for hay to feed the livestock. There are also vegetables such as tatties, neeps, cabbages, cauliflower, carrots, parsnips, beetroot and lettuce. Spring is also time for the sheep-shearing.

Before the crops are harvested, other procedures have to take place. In the case of cabbages, cauliflower and lettuce, the seedlings have to be transplanted and spaced out to give them room to mature. However, with the neeps – the purple and white swedes, and the common yellow and green variety (both of which grow as big as your head – because the seeds were sown in long rows over approximately an acre, all the seeds grew into small turnip seedlings, close together. And being a root vegetable they cannot be transplanted and thrive like a leaf vegetable, so the farmer has the arduous task of thinning out a field full of neep seedlings, and all this has to be done manually with a hoe. The hoeing takes great dexterity and expertise to spacing just right, without leaving more than one at a time, and without wiping the entire crop out. So to speed the process up, and to make things more interesting, neep-hoeing competitions were held on all the farms, over several weeks.

All men and boys, aged from fourteen to forty, competed in this major competition. Each field event was judged separately by independent experts, and the annual champion, runner-up, and third position were all announced at a major gathering held at the village hall on the final Saturday night. Prizes and cups were awarded, and a good time was had by all.

The grain crops and hay were harvested by tractor and binder – before combined harvesters were invented – and gathered into sheaves which were manually loaded onto another tractor and trailer and made into hay stacks. Harvesting was always at the end of summer, round about September. In keeping with tradition, at least two sheaves of corn were displayed in the Kirk next to the pulpit, and everyone was expected to attend on Thanksgiving Sunday in celebrate another year of bountiful harvest. For us, this was straight from the Sunday School to the big Kirk service.

Before our own tattie crop was ready, I would go on my bike to Westermill farm for half a stone of new potatoes. These would be carefully sorted, first by weighing the steel galvanised bucket before adding the tatties. When seven pounds exactly (including the weight of bucket) was reached on the official, hand-held scale, the tatties were duly poured into a small sack. Having paid the going price of a shilling and sixpence for the half stone, I set off with the sack on my handlebars, downhill all the way home fortunately. New tatties were never peeled, just washed and a quick rub over with a scrubbing brush.

Agricultural shows were always big events in the annual farming calendar. The two main ones were held in Kirkwall and St Margaret's Hope and both were held during summer, about a month apart. They were usually two-day events, held at week-ends and in open fields, with all sorts of marquees and tents and all the latest tractors, ploughs and harvesters on show and for sale. This was along with all the prize livestock of cattle, sheep, pigs, hens, geese and even horses and dogs. For us kids there were a number of amusement stalls, and sweets and ice cream to buy. The shows had an exciting carnival atmosphere and it seemed to me that everyone from all over Orkney was in attendance.

The judging and award-giving seemed to go on all the time over the two days, so there were horses, bulls, and cows going around sporting large red, white and blue rosettes, and farmers going around similarly attired. On the evening of the final show-day, a dinner-dance award ceremony was held in the town hall and prizes awarded to the winners in all the categories.

Even in our own village hall in Burray, there was a constant stream of activities and entertainment. This hall was directly across the road from the school, on the opposite corner. The building itself was solidly built, of stone with a slate roof and wooden sash-type windows, and a wooden front door opened into a small porch and then into the main hall. This had windows down the sides, and a raised stage with curtains and a side entrance. Through the hall to the left was a sort of vestibule, or annexe, which was a very big room with a separate kitchen and toilets. The toilets were marked individually ladies and gents and even then had wash-basins and flushing toilets. This vestibule part of the hall had its own solid, wooden side door to the outside, and the whole building was surrounded by a hand-built stone wall approximately five feet high and with an iron gate.

The hall was put to many uses, including being the venue for our picture shows. Every Saturday night there was a show, unless a more important event took priority. The hall was set up with a screen on the stage and six rows of bench seats arranged with the aisle down the middle. The projector was situated at the main door behind us, as we faced the screen. The show was always ninepence and we paid at the door in return for a ticket which was torn off a roll. I think this sort of ticket roll was used for all kinds of events.

The blinds in the hall would be drawn and the lights switched off – with us trying to keep reasonably quiet. The projector whirred into action with a start-up test picture and, once the projector had been focused, there was a burst of sound and the show started. We always had a short cartoon, perhaps Mickey Mouse, Donald Duck or Popeye, before the 'Pathe News' and, finally, the main feature. If we were really lucky this would be in technicolor, but usually it was black and white. The cinema was attended by kids and adults in equal numbers, and since nearly all adults smoked – and probably about half the kids as well – the projector-beam above our heads varied in intensity according to the frequency of pipe and cigarette smokers.

It seemed us kids that smoking was as normal as eating or drinking – just about everyone did it. The rule was that you had to be at least one of the big boys – at least fifteen. Although both my mother and father smoked continually, I couldn't see the point and never really got involved. I was once told that the word 'fags' for cigarettes was an acronym written on wooden crates during the war, meaning 'for a good smoker'. Since I believed everything I was told, I knew that must be true. You could buy cigarettes in packets of ten or twenty, either plain tobacco or the new style with a filter-tip. Popular brands were Capstan, Players or Woodbine, although my mother usually smoked Craven A. My father had a special hand-held roller machine which he used with a green and gold tin of Virginia Tobacco and red or green packs of Rizla papers. The thin white paper was gummed along one edge and, when rolled around the tobacco through the machine, it came out a perfect fag.

Cigarettes were usually lit with Swan or Bluebell matches, or using a petrol-filled brass lighter, with a flint for ignition. Both systems seemed to work fine, even outside in the keen Orkney wind. As kids we collected the picture cards that came in every pack, and we even cut out the pictures on the boxes to hang up in continuous chains. I don't know if smoking was regarded as an expensive sin or addiction, but sometimes if my father ran out I would have to rush down to Douglas's Garage to buy ten Woodbines. When I was nine, ten Woodbines cost one shilling, ten and a ha'penny.

Although Burray had its shops and post office, it did not have a bank. Every Tuesday the Royal Bank of Scotland van would arrive from St Margaret's Hope to set up shop in our village hall annex, with the main hall used as the waiting room. This once-weekly manual banking (before computers were invented) was regarded as adequate, except on the rare occasion when it was considered necessary to go to the Hope or to the Kirkwall main bank direct.

Not all of Orkney's islands can be reached by road, and for the outlying islands that also needed banking services the Royal Bank had a special 'floating' bank – a motor launch – which visited the other important islands once a week – leaving from the Kirkwall Harbour.

Our local South Ronaldsay and Burray doctor, who was resident in the Hope, also set up his consulting rooms/clinic in the village hall on Thursdays (presumably, people in Burray only became ill on Thursdays). However Dr Hooker did make house calls all over the islands of South Ronaldsay and Burray. I recall two occasions when he came to visit me personally.

The first occasion was in the initial week of our six-week school summer holidays, when I jumped off this huge steel buoy that we always played on at the beach. The buoy looked like the body of a fuel tanker truck lying on its round side, with its two circular ends of about six and a half feet in diameter. On the day, three or four of us were playing on the buoy when I jumped off and landed with my foot on the broken end of a glass bottle. In such a dire emergency it was decided that it would be best to get home as fast as possible, along the beach and across the links, with me hobbling and losing a lot of blood along the way.

Once home, someone called for Dr Hooker who got there

in less than half an hour. When he arrived I was lying flat on my back on a chair with some sort of tourniquet around my leg to stop the bleeding, and my left foot raised above a basin of blood. Although still conscious, I was a bit hazy from losing at least half my blood supply, or so it seemed to me.

Dr Hooker was his usual amiable, relaxed self, and seemed to talk and laugh a lot while I was lying there three-quarters dead. He took forever to tackle the emergency before his patient died. With everyone looking on, my mother and the doctor cleaned the wound with warm water and Dettol – no anaesthetic – and the almost mortal wound was finally stitched up. This took three or four stitches, a plaster and a bandage. I was informed that I would probably live, though I still think it was touch-and-go.

My second house-call from Dr Hooker was only a week later when he arrived to check if I was still alive and to remove the stitches, pronounce me officially repaired, and then bandage me back up again.

However, as he was leaving, he noticed that I still had most of my baby teeth. At nine years old, either because this wasn't typical or because he could see potential trouble in the future, he decided to take some pre-emptive measures and pull them all out except for four at the back – two top and two bottom. I asked my usual dentist, Dr Dunnet in Kirkwall, how it was possible that just any passing doctor could pull your teeth out. He explained that Dr Hooker was an ex-Naval doctor, and doctors at sea have to do everything.

Now, having had everything done to me, I was left unable to walk – or eat. As luck would have it this was only the end of the first week of the holidays, so I managed to hobble around on one leg, and to grow some teeth, by the end of the sumer.

Dr Hooker had a habit of asking his patients for any small glass bottles and jars. There was no plastic then, and everything came in jars, bottles, tins and paper pokes. Dr Hooker did his own dispensing and the bottles came in handy. And when you were on the receiving end of a prescription, you got one of his bottles with your name ('Duncan'), ailment ('cough'), and dosage ('two a day after meals'). There was no fancy child-lock seal in those days, and you never really knew what this prescription contained. His prescriptions would be available to be collected at Wylie's shop on the Saturday following the consultation. And, if you were really convincing, you might get a line for one or two days off school.

* * *

Other events that took place in our village hall were often organised by the S.W.R.I. – the Scottish Women's Rural Institute. My mother was a proud member of this staunch league, and wore an official S.W.R.I. badge. My father told me that it stood for 'Silly Women Running Idle'. (Mind you, he also told me that we were members of the 'Wise' Club – the United Kingdom of Great Britain being made up of the Welsh – Irish – Scots and English. I thought this was some sort of claim to fame.)

The S.W.R.I. held a sale of work once or twice a year. Their members baked and made jam, sweets, pickles and wine, and collected new and second-hand goods such as books, clocks, watches, jewellery, toys, household goods, tools, clothes, fruit and vegetables, and even chickens and other livestock. They also had a few raffles and of course, our favourite, the Lucky Dip. A wooden tea-chest full of sawdust was acquired from the boat-yard, and the prize dips were tied to strings, buried at random depths in the sawdust, and for threepence you could choose your string and hope to get lucky. All the profits were used to finance the Institute's work or was donated to various charities.

While still at the Burray School, I got involved in S.W.R.I. whist drives. These were played once a fortnight during autumn and winter. If my mother's whist partner couldn't make it for whatever reason then I was roped into a game. I was considered good at cards, although Granny referred to them as the 'Devil's book'. I actually grew to like playing with the 'old fogeys', although considering these 'fogeys' included my mother and

William Dickson the headmaster, there was probably no one over fifty.

As partners, my mother and I became quite skilled at the game and even came first sometimes. The prizes were good, as I recall. There was a decent torch once – complete with batteries.

Our school concerts were also performed on the stage in the village hall, and although we always went to see them all, I was only ever actually in one – and that was to play the side drum during one of the events. The grown-ups also put on plays and concerts in the hall, and they were always much more interesting and entertaining than our own. Various dances with live music were also held in the hall, played, I thought very professionally, by the locals. This included piano, accordion, fiddle (violin), drums and mouth organ. I don't think anyone had a guitar. These dinner dances included the local Burray agriculture prize-giving awards, a Rabbie Burns night on 25 January, and any weddings and other special occasions.

* * *

As I've said, Orkney is always windy, and sometimes it would get really stormy with very rough seas. On these days we would rush home from school, change into our dungarees or jeans, welly-boots, jerseys and jerkin, and rush down to the beach on our bikes. The beach we favoured was on the exposed North Sea side of the Barrier, about two-thirds of a mile away, and then we'd walk along the beach for the same distance – to discover what had been washed ashore.

This adventure was always exciting – we might find fish boxes, planks of wood, even ladders, ropes, nets and of course, our favourite, the aluminium buoys. We always picked up the valuable flotsam and jetsam to take home. However, when there was too many heavy planks and boxes, we had to leave some of it behind. Now there was an unwritten 'beach code' which allowed the finder to 'lay-up' anything well above the high-water mark on the bank or sand dunes. This was religiously upheld by all. Never in my life have I seen or even heard of any transgression or dispute regarding this code. And so, when you went back a day or even a week later, your spoils would be there intact – exactly where you had left them. I have even seen wood and boxes 'laid-up' for so long that they had become overgrown by grass, but they were still left untouched.

* * *

My granny, Mary Bruce, on my mother's side, was apparently related to the Robert the Bruce in some way, although no one managed to trace this through the family tree – as far as I know. Although Granny lived in the town of St Margaret's Hope on the island of South Ronaldsay, she had originally stayed on the island of Burray, where my mother was born. I could travel the three miles from home by bus, across the Churchill Barrier, from Burray to the Hope to visit her, but from the age of eight I could cycle there on my bike. This meant I could come and go at any time I pleased – although I never travelled such a distance in the dark, or if the weather was really stormy with waves and sea-spray going right over the Barrier. I didn't risk it on days like that.

Visiting Granny was something I really looked forward to. Although St Margaret's Hope was only really a village, to me – as an eight year old – it seemed a big town. The Hope was built on the side of a hill, sloping down to the sea, and Granny lived in a stone-built terraced house, with the front door onto the pavement of the main road. This was directly across the road from the post office, which was situated on the bank overlooking the beach.

When you entered the front door of Granny's house, there was a stone step up into a small entrance landing, with stairs leading to the bedroom, and then more stairs up to the attic. From this ground floor landing there was a door to the left into the living or dining room, with its central range fireplace. Through the living room to the back was the kitchen, scullery, store and toilet – sort of all in one. Although there was a cold water tap, there was no bath or flush toilet. The toilet was a commode or bucket system, and this was only enclosed by my brother Gavin when he started work as an apprentice joiner. I always thought he made a really good job of this toilet enclosure with its wooden frame, and walls panelled on both sides with hardboard and Masonite, fitted as it was with a hinged and locking door.

The back door led out to a small, stone yard with ten steps up to the garden. This may have seemed odd, but the whole village was built sloping up from the sea to the top of the brae, and Granny's house was at the bottom of the hill and everything else, including her garden, rose up quite steeply. The garden had a central path leading to a door in the back stone wall. Granny had the garden and washing-line on the left side of this path, while her neighbours had the right side. Each garden was quite big, about thirty yards by six, with really rich, black soil, and Granny was able to grow tatties, carrots, beetroot, onions, peas, lettuce, cabbages, various flowers, and of course rhubarb.

The door in the wall at the top led out onto an alleyway and into the next street – the Top Road. This door was never locked as there was never any problems with trespassing or crime.

Granny's village was quite big, with the school at the top of the next hill, and the show-grounds across the road. At the bottom of the school brae was the blacksmith's shop. Although they did shoe some horses, the smithy was in production everyday for all the making and repairing of all sorts of iron and steel goods.

Along the road from the blacksmith was the small pier – Spence's Pier, next to Spence's General Store. Mr Herbert Spence, the owner, was a strictly religious man, and as bairns, we sort of regarded him as miserly, but keen to do business. We would go in and enquire about paint, and after several minutes end up ordering a pint or even gallon of tartan paint. We would also request a seat for a wheelbarrow, or other such nonsense. Although this must have annoyed Mr Spence, he never showed it, and carried on trying to get us to buy something, anything.

My mother managed to provoke him, however, when she went in to buy twenty Craven A cigarettes, and he had an uncharacteristic outburst about never having the 'craving' or the 'A'! She never went back to his shop.

However, I did buy one of my first pocket penknives from Spence's shop. It was a trade-marked Nest Knife, with two blades. As Spence assured me, 'Nest knifes are the best knives. They last till they're lost'. Now since I couldn't live without a pocket knife, this resounding guarantee clinched the deal.

The Spence Pier was used mainly by the fishing and lobster boats. About a third of a mile around the bay, there was another bigger pier – this was only used by cargo and passenger ships, although not very often.

The Hope also had a post office, bank, two hotels and bars, a fish and chip shop cum restaurant, and Herbert MacKenzie's (apparently no relation to us) Watch & Clock Supply and Repair shop – where you could buy a good pocket watch for ten shillings. There was also a Kirk, village hall and another four general shops, Guthrie's butcher shop, a diesel-petrol station, and two main streets of terraced houses, stone-built with slate roofs, all two or three storeys high, and lots of free-standing houses, even some down on the beach. The roads were well tarred and the pavement made from stone.

Public toilets were situated in a stone building right down on the sea front. There were four of each, for men and women, with open-fronted cubicles complete with long drops and wooden seats built right over the beach, and flushed by the high tide.

When the tide came in, you could stand on the sea front, or at the walls of the houses and watch all sorts of fish and crabs swimming around. However, all sorts of household and slop bucket rubbish was discarded into sea like a natural waste-disposal system. Even Guthrie's butcher shop across the road from Granny used to throw out all sorts of bones and scraps straight onto the rocky part of this beach. This attracted all manner of rodents (especially rats), as well as seagulls and other birds.

Except for the main towns in Orkney at that time, and then only in a limited way, there was no council-organised rubbish collection service. We had our own hospital and ambulance service, doctors and nurses, fire brigade, police force and even a court house and prison, but the collection and disposal of rubbish was always a bit haphazard. Anything that couldn't be eaten by the pigs and hens, and which could be burned, was either incinerated inside in your fireplace, or outside in a bonfire once or twice a week. All the ash was then buried. Cans, bottles and just about anything that wouldn't burn, was generally dumped onto the various beaches, or even thrown over the Churchill Barriers.

This seemed to work quite well, considering Orkney consists of approximately seventy islands and has a total population of never more than twenty thousand folk. And with all the burning and dumping that went on, there never seemed to be any concern about the effect on wildlife or the environment.

Sometimes I stayed overnight at Granny's and I gave her a hand here and there, or did a few jobs like going up to Doull's or Robertson's shop, or weeding in the garden, or digging up the potatoes – which were delicious when boiled straight out the ground. I also used to do a spot of painting – like the outside doors and windows, or the iron railings. Sometimes I climbed up on the small back-roof and scraped off the moss and cleaned the gutters.

When I didn't have work to do, I was free to go fishing and I made friends with some of the local boys, and one girl called K. I thought this was really strange, having just one letter for a name, although it was explained to me that her name was actually Kay or Katrina or something.

At Granny's house, I liked to sit around the fire and listen to the wireless or just talk. I could make toast on the extra-long toasting fork, although she told me it was really just scorched bread I was making. Granny, on the other hand, could make really good toast in the oven.

As I remember, she cooked quite differently to my mother –

in a very old-fashioned way. Some of my favourites were fresh herrings fried in oatmeal, fried cod roe, dried salted fish, boiled and served with new tatties and dripping fat and clapshot – boiled potatoes and turnips mashed together – steak and kidney, liver and onions, and scotch broth, oatcakes, scones and bere bannocks. Rhubarb was also a regular feature. We all grew it – or rather, it grew by itself. Rhubarb would defy anything or anyone to stop it.

For milk, Granny set an empty bottle on the front door step every night, and a new full bottle was left there early in the morning.

Granny had a fat, black cat called Korky, whose main job was rodent control, although it was good at eating all the scraps and leftovers. I don't think Granny ever bought a tin of commercial cat food – I don't think she really believed there was such a thing.

Her friend, Jock Omand visited every now and then, usually between nine in the morning and noon. Sometimes he would stay for dinner. Jock and Granny would talk non-stop, discussing things or just plain arguing. One day I was lucky enough to be there when they were 'discussing' a ten-bob note which Jock gave to Granny, but she said she didn't want it and gave it back. After a few interchanges of the note, she settled the argument by giving it to me and told me to keep it. I didn't need to be told twice. That settled the argument, and made me rich, all at the same time.

When at home or with Granny, I had to take a teaspoon of cod liver oil every day – and that was when I had nothing wrong with me. This ritual was modernised much later when it changed from liquid to capsules. Capsules weren't quite so bad if you swallowed them quickly, and so I got very good it. If I had any ailments, such as spots, a rash or a temperature, then it was a dessert-spoon of black treacle and yellow sulphur powder, which of course cured every ailment ever known, and some that hadn't even been invented. For a really bad cold, cough or flu, I would get a hot toddy (honey, whisky and hot water) in a glass to drink, then straight to bed with a hot water bottle. When we were very young it was gripe water, rosehip syrup and Vicks Vapour Rub that prevented, or cured, everything. For any other ailments, like cuts, bruises, stings or sores, there was always Dettol, Germoline, Calamine Lotion or plasters. For boils we used bread poultices, bicarbonate of soda to kill warts, and we washed our hair with Coal Tar shampoo. If, on a very rare occasion, none of the above worked, we went to the doctor.

Living in Orkney and doing what I did on a daily basis, I was prone to cuts and bruises and bashed black fingernails. This seemed to be regarded as normal, and I always had one or two plasters stuck on here and there. However one day, when I was about twelve, I realised for the first time in memory that I had no plasters, no cuts or bruises, and no chapped fingernails. This felt and looked so good that I endeavoured to avoid injury in the future.

Not everything was medicinal. I particularly remember that we had Creamola Foam to drink. This came in various flavours – orange, lemon and strawberry were the favourites. Creamola Foam was a powder that came in a small tin. A teaspoon of this in a glass of cold water was as good as any bottled lemonade or cola.

My mum and granny used to knit, and if we went to visit my Aunt Aggie, she was always knitting too. It wasn't as though they did knitting instead of something else, knitting was a bit like breathing and it was just something they did while doing everything else. I think they could sit and talk and knit, read and listen to the wireless and knit, knit, cook and wash dishes, knit, wash clothes and hang them out to dry, and knit. Their knitting was just endless, so I suppose I shouldn't be surprised that we always had all sorts of knitted jerseys and socks. My favourite, when I was four or five, was my Fair Isle knitted woollen jersey. Who knitted it, I never found out, as there was all this knitting going on non-stop. I'm amazed the sheep could keep up with it. There would be hanks and reels and balls of wool everywhere, and even emergency supplies of all the right colours for repair jobs. Between the darning and the knitting, the work never ended. I also think the S.W.R.I. members stockpiled their knitted jerseys and socks for their sales of work, and for Christmas and birthdays and any surprise emergencies you might think of.

By the time I was twelve, Ian was sixteen and had left school and gone to work in Edinburgh. Gavin was fourteen and would leave school at sixteen to start work in the Hope as an apprentice joiner. When Gavin got a job with the main local joinery and carpentry company, he sometimes stayed with Granny, but usually he travelled the three miles each way on his N.S.U. motorbike (really a moped). Although N.S.U. set a world speed record of over two hundred miles an hour in 1956, Gavin reached a more sedate speed of just over fifty in 1966.

I tried his bike a few times, and it was amazing how fast you could zip around. You could get across the Barrier and back in no time. I decided that as soon as possible I must trade my bicycle in for something like this, and I eventually did.

Colin was now eight and my baby sister Fiona four. Colin was into his third year at our old Burray School and Fiona was about to start. It didn't seem that long ago that I would visit Aunt Aggie's, or go to the shops with my mother, pushing Fiona in the green pram with the fold-down hood, complete with the milk bottles and rattles and baby paraphernalia. Pushing the pram was very easy, and since Fiona would be facing me she would laugh and talk. When we got to the shops, or Aunt Aggie's, or wherever we were going, Fiona would get out and walk. If she got tired on the way home, it was back into the pram for a sleep. Soon Colin and Fiona would be old enough to take over most of the hen and cat duties.

I suppose I was really becoming the older brother now, although it never really seemed like that to me. I was too caught up in my own learning and studies, trying to decide what I wanted to do with my life, or could do, now that I would soon be reaching school-leaving age. Somehow I never really got the chance to discuss with Colin and Fiona how their own school lives and learning were going. I knew though that Fiona and the other children were still required to recite, as we were, 'The Lord's Prayer' every morning, standing in order at their school desks:

Our father which art in heaven
Hallowed be thy name
Thy kingdom come
Thy will be done on earth, as it is in heaven
Give us each day our daily bread
And forgive us our debts
As we forgive our debtors
And lead us not into temptation
But deliver us from evil
For thine is the kingdom
The power and the glory
Forever and ever. Amen.

It is easy to look back now and say what I could have, and should have, done, as far as school was concerned. Perhaps, more importantly, I might have realised that such a great and interesting opportunity was made available to us, and all three of us were deprived by not taking advantage of the education on offer at the time.

EPILOGUE

I LEFT SCHOOL at sixteen and in 1965 joined the Royal Air Force at Aberdeen and moved to Staffordshire. It turned out to be not what I wanted, so it was back to Orkney for me.

In August of the same year I headed to Glasgow and joined H. M. Fulton Limited as an apprentice electrician, which lasted until 1970. I enjoyed Glasgow immensely, and my studies, and I gained my motorbike, car and heavy-duty truck driving licences while I was there.

Then it was the Army, and I joined the 15th (Scottish) Army Paratroopers Battalion for four years of flying, parachuting, fighting, shooting and demolition. I got my 'wings' in the first year with approximately twelve jumps from both planes and helicopters. It was a great opportunity for travel throughout Britain and Europe.

In August 1971 I left for South Africa, now aged 22, and flew B.O.A.C. to Johannesburg armed with my electrical qualification and City and Guilds Certificate. There I worked as Electrical Supervisor at the new Kempston Park Hospital before becoming Service Manager at the Metter–Pingon crane and excavator company. I eventually left to form my own electrical and mechanical engineering business before becoming a consultant for electrical cranes and hoists.

In 1980 I moved to Botswana as National Service Manager for the Blackwood Hodge earth-moving and lifting company, before going to Cape Town to work for Davy S.A. (Morris Cranes/Crane Aid Services). Having worked with the South African National Life Assurance Company, and become a financial consultant, estate agent and electrical/water purification adviser, I now consider myself well and truly desk-bound!

But it hasn't been all work – other life events include getting married on 6 November 1976 to Elizabeth Moir in the old stone church in Benoni, near Johannesburg (complete with a Scottish piper in full traditional regalia). Our son, David, was born in Johannesburg in November 1980. After thirty years of marriage, Elizabeth and I were divorced. Since then I have lived with Vi Smith as my partner.

Outside work and family and continuing my studies, I have been involved in the Round Table organisations of both Central Africa and South Africa, and the Sea Scouts when David was growing up in Cape Town.

My philosophy – having travelled throughout the world – is to live life according to the three 'Es' – Enthusiasm, Energy and Expectation. To achieve what you want out of life, you need to be inspired with Enthusiasm, have the Energy to proceed, and have the Expectation of fulfilment – then, anything is possible.

And, for myself, I'd say that to play a game of bridge often and to laugh every day, is also important – although not necessarily at the same time!

GLOSSARY

This selective list contains only those terms found in the text that may need explanation:

Ba' game, traditional ball game played in Kirkwall on New Year's Day

bere bannocks, baked scone made with bere barley

B.O.A.C, British Overseas Airways Corporation

bodkin, a blunt needle with a large eye for drawing tape or ribbon through a loop or hem

bushel, a measure of capacity used for corn, fruit, *etc.*, containing four pecks or eight gallons

clapshot, mashed potato and turnip dish with chopped chives or spring onions

comper, puffer fish

creels, a basket, esp. a fish basket

curly doddies, plants, such as clover, with rounded flower-head

D.D.T., dichlorodiphenyl-trichloroethane, an organophosphate pesticide

dooking, the act of plunging, dipping or bobbing, eg, for apples at Halloween

drookeled, soaked with water

dunter, one who beats or knocks

firkin, a measure equal to the fourth part of a barrel, nine gallons.

the Hope, St Margaret's Hope

neepie lantern, lantern made out of a hollowed-out turnip, esp. at Hallowe'en

Nissan/Nissen hut, a tunnel-shaped hut made of corrugated iron with a cement floor

partan, edible crab

peedie, small

roost, rust

simmit, vest

slughs, pea-pods

spoots, razor clams; also artificial conduit for water (e.g. on a roof)

Stillson spanners, a type of adjustable wrench

tawse, belt